A Sweet and
Glorious Land

George Gissing, photographed two years
before leaving for Italy on the 1897 journey
that led to the writing of *By the Ionian Sea*.
Photo by Mendelssohn

A Sweet and Glorious Land

Revisiting the Ionian Sea

John Keahey

Thomas Dunne Books
St. Martin's Press ✼ New York

THOMAS DUNNE BOOKS.
An imprint of St. Martin's Press.

A SWEET AND GLORIOUS LAND: REVISITING THE IONIAN SEA. Copyright © 2000 by
John Keahey. All rights reserved. Printed in the United States of America. No
part of this book may be used or reproduced in any manner whatsoever without
written permission except in the case of brief quotations embodied in critical
articles or reviews. For information, address St. Martin's Press, 175 Fifth Avenue,
New York, N.Y. 10010.

Design by Nancy Resnick

Library of Congress Cataloging-in-Publication Data

Keahey, John.
    A sweet and glorious land : revisiting the Ionian Sea / John Keahey.
        p. cm.
    Includes bibliographical references.
    ISBN 0-312-24205-0
    1. Italy, Southern—Description and travel. 2. Keahey, John—Journeys—
Italy, Southern. 3. Gissing, George, 1857-1903—Journeys—Italy, Southern.
I. Title: Subtitle: Revisiting the Ionian Sea. II. Title.

DG821 .K43 2000
917.5'704929—dc21   00-027934

First Edition: June 2000

10   9   8   7   6   5   4   3   2   1

For Connie-Lou Disney

All the faults of the Italian people are whelmed in forgiveness as soon as their music sounds under the Italian sky. One remembers all they have suffered, all they have achieved in spite of wrong. Brute races have flung themselves, one after another, upon this sweet and glorious land; conquest and slavery, from age to age, have been the people's lot. Tread where one will, the soil has been drenched with blood.

George Gissing
By the Ionian Sea: Notes of a Ramble in Southern Italy, 1901

Gissing, far left, in Rome early in 1898, a few
months after returning from southern Italy
and his Ionian Sea adventure. With, left to
right, Ernest W. Hornung, brother-in-law of
Arthur Conan Doyle; Doyle; and H. G. Wells.
Photographer unknown

Contents

Contents

NORTH

ETRUSCANS

Tiber River

MARCHE

UMBRIA

I T A L Y

ABRUZZI

LAZIO

Rome

A D R I A T I C   S E A

Via Latina

Via Appia

MOLISE

CAMPANIA

Via Traiana

Cannae

Cápua

Bari

PUGLIA

Cumae

Naples

Salerno

Via Appia

Ischia

Bríndisi

Capri

BASILICATA

Tàranto

Poseidonia/
Paestum

Via Popilia

A3

Skidros

Metaponto

SOUTHERN ITALY
Magna Graecia

Laos

Gulf of Táranto

Trebisacce

Sybaris/Thurii/Copia

T Y R R H E N I A N   S E A

S107

Crati R.

Páola

S106

Cosenza

CALABRIA

Kroton/Cotrone/Crotone

Capo Colonna

Catanzaro

Schilletion/Scylacium/Squillace

A3

Palermo

Messina

Riace

Rhegion/Rhegium/Reggio di Calabria

SICILY

Cátania

I O N I A N   S E A

Agrigento

Syrakusai/Siracusa

Steve Baker, Salt Lake City

Chronology

c. 753	Traditional, perhaps mythical, founding of Rome by Romulus
c. 750	Homer's *Iliad* first written down First Greek colony in Magna Graecia (Great Greece), or southern Italy, believed established on modern Ischia, in Gulf of Naples.
740	Cumae (modern Cuma), earliest Greek colony on Italian mainland, established
720	Sybaris (later named Thurii by Greeks and still later renamed Copia by Romans) in the far south of Italy founded by Achaean Greeks near the mouth of the river Crati Rhegion (Roman Rhegium, modern Reggio di Calabria) founded by Chalcidian Greeks
710	Kroton (modern Crotone, known as Cotrone from the Middle Ages until C.E. 1928) founded by Achaean Greeks
706	Taras (Roman Tarentum, modern Taranto), founded by Spartan Greeks
c. 700	Palatine settlement in Rome expands. The Forum, between the Palatine and the Capitoline Hills, is laid out as a public meeting place Metapontion (Roman Metapontum, modern Metaponto) established along the Bradano River as buffer colony between Taras (Taranto) and Sybaris
c. 650	Rise of the "tyrants" in Greece First Greek coins and rise of lyric Greek poetry
c. 600	Foundation of Greek colony at Massilia (modern Marseilles in southern France) Greek colony at Neapolis (modern Naples) founded by colonists from Cumae, ten miles to the northwest

	Sybaris establishes colony at Poseidonia, later renamed Paestum by Romans in 273 B.C.E. Development of Latin script
c. 530	Greek mathematician and philosopher Pythagoras active in southern Italy
510	Sybaris destroyed by fellow colonists from nearby Kroton
509	Last of kings expelled from Rome; the Roman Republic founded
c. 485	First western historian Herodotus, born at Halicarnassus in what is now southwestern Turkey; dies about 425, either in Thurii, in southern Italy, or in Pella, in Macedonia, north of mainland Greece
480–460	Carthage expands African territory
460–430	Herodotus writes *Histories*
c. 479–338	Period of Greek classical culture
444	Colony of Thurii built by Greek colonists on site of destroyed Sybaris Cumae overrun by Italic tribes
410	Carthage invades Sicily
c. 380	Roman expansion in Italy begins Romans conquer Cumae
341–295	Rome wages war with native peoples through much of the Italian peninsula; conflicts range from Latin War through Battle of Sentinum, establishing Rome's supremacy in Italy
336	Assassination of Philip at Pella in Macedonia; Alexander the Great (356–323), his son, succeeds to the Macedonian throne as Alexander III of Macedonia
c. 336–31	Greek Hellenic period

Chronology

C.E.

14–37	Tiberius emperor of Rome
393	Olympic Games in Greece abolished
395	Division of Roman Empire between East, in Constantinople (now Istanbul), and West, in Rome
410	Alaric the Visigoth (western Goth) sacks Rome for the third time, hastening the eventual fall of the (western) Roman Empire; dies in Consentia/Cosenza and is believed buried in the bed of the Busento River
476	Last Roman emperor in the West deposed; replaced by a barbarian king
489–493	The Ostrogoths (eastern Goths) under Theodoric invade and conquer Italy
490	Cassiodorus born in area around modern-day Squillace in southern Italy, dies about 585; works with his father, who serves Theodoric
568	Germanic Lombards take over northern half of the Italian peninsula
c. 820	Muslims from North Africa conquer Sicily
962	Germanic king invades Italy and is crowned emperor in Rome
982	Germanic peoples defeated by the Arabs when they attempt to conquer southern Italy
1072	Normans (descendants of the Vikings) capture Palermo in Sicily
1130	Norman ruler is crowned king of Sicily, Calabria, and Apulia (modern Puglia)

1442	Naples falls to the ruler of Sicily, Alfonso V of Aragon, who in 1443 assumes the title King of the Two Sicilies, that is, of Sicily and Naples
1504	Spain assumes control of the Kingdom of Naples, which, for several years around the end of the fifteenth century, has been caught up in the struggles of foreign powers fighting to dominate Italy; Naples and Sicily are ruled by Spanish viceroys for two centuries
1527	The out-of-control armies of Emperor Charles V enter Rome and sack the city. Within a week, troops pillage and destroy thousands of churches, palaces, and houses; this event marks Rome's demise as a center of the Renaissance
1706–1708	The Kingdom of Naples comes under the influence of the Austrian Habsburgs, along with Milan and Sardinia
1734	Don Carlos de Borbón (later King Charles III of Spain) is granted cultural patronage at Naples and establishes the Bourbon fortunes in Italy
1735	Austria cedes Naples and Sicily–the "Kingdom of the Two Sicilies"–to the Bourbons; during the eighteenth century, in the spirit of "enlightened despotism," the rulers sponsor reforms to rectify social and political injustices and to modernize the state
1796–1799	The French, under Napoleon, invade Italy, beginning the era of the Italian Republic
1802	Napoleon Bonaparte becomes president of the Italian Republic; Milan is his capital
1805	Napoleon declares himself king of Italy his sister Paolina eventually becomes ruler of the duchies of Parma, Guastalla, and Piacenza

1806	After first annexing the Kingdom of the Two Sicilies to France, Napoleon then declares it independent and installs his brother Joseph as king
1808	Joseph is transferred to Spain, and Napoleon gives Naples to his brother-in-law Joachim Murat; under the French, Naples is modernized by the abolition of feudalism and the introduction of a uniform legal code, and Murat is deservedly popular as king; Napoleon also installs his young son as king of Rome
c. 1815	Napoleon's influence begins to wane throughout the Italian peninsula; Bourbon rule is restored in Naples, and the Kingdom of the Two Sicilies aligns with the conservative states of Europe
1820	Sicilian people win constitutional concessions from their Bourbon rulers, as well as further concessions in 1848, when Sicily tries to win independence from Bourbon rule in Naples; the kingdom's poor political and economic condition leads to its easy collapse in the mid-nineteenth century just prior to Italian unification
1849	Vittorio Emanuele II becomes king of Sardinia
1857	George R. Gissing, Victorian novelist and short story writer, born in Wakefield, Yorkshire, England, November 22
1860	Garibaldi conquers Sicily, then conquers southern Italy
1861	Kingdom of Italy proclaimed under Vittorio Emanuele II; first elections of Italian Parliament; bandits (brigands) dominate much of South
1865	Capital of the Kingdom of Italy moves from Turin to Florence

Chronology

1870	Rome proclaimed capital
1878	Vittorio Emanuele II dies; succession of Umberto I
1888	Gissing's first wife, Nell, dies in London; Gissing travels to Paris, Naples, Rome, Florence, and Venice
1889	Gissing travels to Greece and Naples, and while in Naples suffers from the first bout of a lung disease, probably emphysema, that will kill him fourteen years later
1891	Gissing marries Edith Underwood, permanently separating from her in 1897, just before leaving for his third and final trip to Italy
1897	Gissing arrives in Italy on September 23, landing in Milan; he settles in Siena to write a critical study of Charles Dickens, which he completes and sends to England on November 6; befriends nineteen-year-old American journalist BrianBorú Dunne; returns briefly to Rome, and then goes on to Naples, where he begins the journey that leads to the writing of *By the Ionian Sea—Notes of a Ramble in Southern Italy*; returns to Rome via Naples and Monte Cassino on December 15
1898	During January, Gissing works in Rome on proofs of the Dickens book; socializes with Dunne, Arthur Conan Doyle, H. G. Wells, and others; leaves April 12 for Berlin and, eventually, England, where he meets Gabrielle Fleury
1899	Gissing moves to Paris to live with Gabrielle, later moving with her to the South of France and living in Ciboure, near Saint-Jean-de-Luz, from mid-1902 to mid-1903; from mid-1903 until his death in December 1903, he and Gabrielle live in Ispoure, France, close to Saint-Jean Pied-de-Port

1900	Umberto I assassinated; Vittorio Emanuele III becomes king
1901	*By the Ionian Sea* published in England
1903	Gissing dies December 28 and is buried in Saint-Jean-de-Luz
1919	Fascists organize in Milan
1925	Mussolini appointed prime minister of Italy by Vittorio Emanuele III
1935	Italian troops, as part of Mussolini's drive to create a new Roman Empire, invade Abyssinia (Ethiopia) in North Africa
1936	Italy conquers Abyssinia; Mussolini creates the Italian Empire; Rome-Berlin Axis is inaugurated
1940	Italy declares war on France and Great Britain
1943	Fascist Party dissolved; Italy surrenders to Allies; much of Italy is immediately occupied by the Germans; Allies land at Salerno after capturing Sicily
1944	Allies liberate Rome
1945	Anti-Fascist Carlo Levi publishes *Cristo si è fermato a Eboli* (Christ Stopped at Eboli), his memoir of the year he was exiled to southern Italy before World War II
1946	Despite strong opposition by southern Italians, who have monarchist and authoritarian sentiments, Italians vote—twelve million to ten million—to abolish the monarchy, which supported the Fascists
1948–1964	Prewar industrial production levels are achieved by 1948, and the country enjoys industrial growth rates of more than 8 percent per annum. In fewer than two decades, the country is transformed

	from a largely agricultural backwater into one of the world's most dynamic industrial nations; this is referred to as Italy's "economic miracle"
1958	*Il Gattopardo* (The Leopard), a historical novel about life and culture in mid-nineteenth century Sicily, is published a year after the death of its author, Giuseppe Tomasi di Lampedusa; it is his only novel and brings Lampedusa international recognition
c. 1960s	Archaeologists intensify efforts to excavate ruins in southern Italy that are eventually identified as Greek-Roman cities of Sybaris/Thurii/Copia, built one on top of the other
c. 1970s	Italian *Brigate Rosse*, or Red Brigades—an extreme left-wing terrorist organization—gains notoriety for kidnappings, murders, and sabotage; its self-proclaimed aim is to undermine the Italian state and pave the way for a Marxist upheaval led by a "revolutionary proletariat"
c. 1980s	The Italian Mafia networks controlled from southern Italy continue their heavy involvement in extortion rackets and government contracts, but increasingly control most of the world's heroin trade; much publicized trials of Mafia leaders from 1986 onward succeed in imprisoning some of the leaders
1992–Present	Investigating magistrates in Milan begin uncovering a series of bribery scandals. The city becomes known as *Tangentopoli* (Bribesville), and under *Mani pulite* (Operation Clean Hands) many leading politicians, civil servants, and businessmen are arrested

A Sweet and Glorious Land

Introduction

Sometime during the early fall of 1997, I read a newspaper article about the death of Lady Diana, Princess of Wales. It mentioned paparazzi, the celebrity photographers who pursued her on the night of her death in a car crash in Paris. A short article, placed adjacent to the one I had been reading, caught my attention. It told of the origin of the word *paparazzi*, about how a celebrity photographer in Federico Fellini's great movie *La dolce vita* was named Paparazzo, and how the name, in its Italian plural with an *i* substituted for the singular ending *o* and with a lowercase *p*, was used to denote all such photographers during and after the celebrity-ridden 1960s.

Fellini and his scriptwriter, the article said, got the name from a travel narrative, first published in 1901, by the Victorian writer George Gissing: *By the Ionian Sea—Notes of a Ramble in Southern Italy*. The book's Italian edition is titled *Sulle rive dello Ionio—Un vittoriano al Sud* (Along the Ionian Coast—A Victorian in the South).

I did not, and still do not, care about paparazzi, but being an

Italophile, I wanted to locate a copy of *By the Ionian Sea*, read it, and add it to my collection of books on Italy. It was a passing thought. I was buying and reading everything I could find about Italy, especially nonfiction travel and expatriate accounts. I was going through a spate of books that seemed to hash over the same themes: They were about the better-known Italian North, or about the Mafia; or about Americans, Central Europeans, or Britons buying and restoring farmhouses in Tuscany, then writing books about their experiences and introducing readers to "a colorful cast of characters." A handful—such as Eric Newby's *A Small Place in Italy* and his *Love and War in the Apennines*, along with Paolo Tullio's *North of Naples, South of Rome* and Harry Clifton's *On the Spine of Italy: A Year in the Abruzzi*—are superb, capturing realistic insights into the Italian people.

Some books extol the comfortable life that foreigners of means can have among Italians. Few, I noticed—except in books about the Mafia—were writing about the poorer, economically depressed South, beyond Naples.

I eventually came across an edition of Gissing's work—a well-used 1986 trade edition—at my favorite local bookseller's. I brought the thin paperback home and placed it at the bottom of the stack of books on my bed stand. It was late November 1997 by the time I worked my way down to *By the Ionian Sea* and discovered I was reading one of the most enchanting travel narratives I had come across in years of seeking out such books.

At one moment, halfway through my reading of this classic, I turned to my wife and said that I wanted to visit Italy and follow in the footsteps Gissing made in 1897 during his third and final trip to Italy: from Naples where he boarded the coastal steamer south to Paola; and from there, in a horse-drawn carriage, through the Calabrian mountains to Cosenza. From

Cosenza, he went by train to Taranto and, using a combination of trains and carriages, made it all the way to Reggio di Calabria. It was a journey that covered much of the foot of Italy, principally along the coastal instep of the Ionian Sea.

I wanted to see, one hundred years after Gissing, how these ancient lands looked. They had been settled for millennia by native Italic peoples and then colonized by the Greeks long before the Romans arrived.

His book was not a diary and the chapters were not dated, but I had the sense the journey must have taken him several weeks, if not a few months. To be sure, I called my rare-book dealer, who found an out-of-print copy of *George Gissing—A Critical Biography*, by Jacob Korg.

This same dealer also found a first edition of *By the Ionian Sea*, published in 1901, and the book dazzled me. It is bound in pale-colored linen, its spine darkened from years of sitting on a bookshelf in a house that must have been heated by a coal furnace or a peat fire. Its creamy pages are deeply embossed with printing that could only have been done with an old letterpress. Periodically a page would be devoted to a full-color reproduction of a watercolor of an Italian scene, the plate covered, for its protection, by a translucent tissue. Gissing's simple drawings of peasant dress, water jugs, and the like punctuated the narrative.

I reread the book, using this first edition. Then I got on the Internet and found that according to the Library of Congress there have been eight or nine U.S. editions of the book over the years. The book has almost always been available in one edition or another since its turn-of-the-century debut.

I also found several Web sites dedicated to George Gissing. There is even a quarterly journal—*The Gissing Journal*—devoted to scholarly works about his life. In this journal I found not one, but two articles detailing Gissing's connection with paparazzi!

Despite my earlier guess that his trip took months, Gissing's biography said that he made the journey into southern Italy, his Magna Graecia, over what appears to be only a one-month period, from early November to early December 1897. His diary reports that Gissing spent his fortieth birthday, November 22, 1897, in the South, while visiting Taranto, a milestone he did not mention in his book. His birthday, just one year short of the age at which his father had died when young George was barely a teenager, came just before his visit to the town then known as Cotrone, and today as Crotone. There George became ill and, at least in his mind, lay near death in his shabby hotel bed, wreathed in sweat and suffering fevered hallucinations. He described his hallucinations immediately after his recovery, according to biographer Korg, in a diary entry dated November 29, 1897.

It was about this time—sometime during the last two weeks of November 1997 and one hundred years to the month of his journey—that I decided to act upon my first inclination and actually follow in Gissing's footsteps. I would go in March 1998, a little more than three months later. I had spent several springs and some falls traveling in Italy. Spending March in the south, I figured, would be delightful. A wonderful excuse for another trip!

The journal I kept of the trip, while nothing like Gissing's detailed diary, became the seed for this book. I conjured up the idea precisely one hundred years to the moment of his travels, and retraced his route one hundred years and three months later. My most-used modes of transportation were the same— trains and foot-power—with the exception of the few jaunts

Gissing made by carriage and the overnight trip in a coastal steamer from Naples to Paola.

When I was not studying maps or guidebooks, I was reading Gissing's short stories and one of his last books, *The Private Papers of Henry Ryecroft*, which many scholars believe is a slightly fictional autobiography. I hoped it would give me insight into the inner workings of this lonely, chronically depressed author who seemed to yearn for inner peace—or perhaps escape—as he walked over the ruins of what used to be glorious cities established so long ago in what was, and continues to be, the economically depressed South of Italy.

I understood that feeling. I recalled that in the mid-1980s, during a particularly painful period of my own life, I stood in a Paris street, in front of the first apartment of American writer Ernest Hemingway. As I stared at its facade, I longed to be transported magically to the early 1920s and see the cobblestones he walked on and the goatherd he saw clicking down those stones with his flock, delivering freshly pulled milk in a bucket on a rope to Hemingway's upstairs neighbor lady. I opened my eyes, as I now suspect Gissing did on such occasions, and found myself right where I had started, in the here and now.

Like Gissing, I met friends in Rome before and after my 1998 southern ramble. He had returned there on December 15, 1897, following a leisurely five-day journey from Reggio, on the far southern edge of Calabria; through Naples for one last look; and then a brief two-day stopover at the monastery at Monte Cassino, occupied four decades later by Germans and destroyed by Allied bombing during World War II.

He stayed on in Rome for four months of socializing, sightseeing, and correcting proofs of his critical study of the works of Charles Dickens. Gissing had finished the manuscript in Siena, a Tuscan city northeast of Rome, just a few weeks before he headed south. The proofs of the Dickens book had caught up with him in the midst of his Ionian Sea adventure.

In Rome, he helped arrange lodgings to house his good friends H. G. Wells and Wells's wife, Catherine. Gissing also renewed an acquaintance with a budding, nineteen-year-old American journalist, BrianBorú Dunne, with whom Gissing had shared lodgings in Siena a few months earlier. Decades after Gissing's death, Dunne wrote a remarkable memoir, edited later by three Gissing scholars and published in 1999, about his friendship with Gissing and their Italian days together (*With Gissing in Italy: The Memoirs of BrianBorú Dunne*).

It must have been a heady time for the young American Dunne, who suddenly found himself in the presence of Gissing, Wells, and, later, Arthur Conan Doyle—three giants of late Victorian literature. In 1959, when Dunne was a frail old man living in Santa Fe, New Mexico, he was visited by English newspaperman Anthony Curtis. Dunne recalled having lunch in Rome with Wells, who had just published *War of the Worlds*, and Gissing, fresh from his return from the Ionian Sea. Later, Dunne took the famous pair to his room. Curtis records Dunne's recollections of the moment: "As they climbed the five flights of stairs . . . Wells paused to say, 'Now here's a young man [Dunne] who wants to write. Here I am who have written a little,' then, pointing to Gissing: 'And there is someone who has mastered thc art.' "

In addition to the frenetic period in Rome of socializing and proofreading the Dickens work, Gissing scoured the city, laying the groundwork for what would be his final work, *Veranilda*, a romance set in Rome shortly after the Western Empire's downfall. He never finished the book's last five chapters, dying in France in 1903. His death came two years after *By the Ionian Sea* was published, and a year or so before *Veranilda* was published in unfinished form.

I worked on this book during most of 1998, realizing after plowing through a mass of additional reading that I had to return to southern Italy for two more weeks of seeking out places I missed earlier. During that first journey I had traveled almost exclusively by train, and did not, for example, go over the mountain road Gissing traveled between Paola and Cosenza, or up into Squillace, several miles away from its train station on the Ionian coast. These places required visits if Gissing's journey was to be retraced properly.

In January 1999, friend and fellow Italophile and author Paul Paolicelli and I headed by car into the Calabrian hills. He read aloud from Gissing's account in between glances at a detailed Touring Club Italiano road map, while I drove. He also took many of the photographs that grace these pages.

In writing this book, the only literary license I have taken is occasionally to combine the two journeys as one. The automobile journeys to Paestum, through the mountains between Paola and Cosenza, to Squillace, to the archaeological dig at Sybaris/Thurii/Copia, and my time at Capo Colonna came during the January 1999 trip. Everything else took place in March–April 1998.

This book, like Gissing's account, is a personal narrative and a work of journalism, not a footnoted history or a scholarly work. All of the knowledge I pass on comes from my own experiences of observing Italians and from traveling through Italy for the past thirteen years, or from other writers, ranging from the ancient historians Herodotus and Livy to modern historians, archaeologists, Gissing scholars, and journalists. They all wrote in a way that allows us to appreciate and understand either George Gissing or this ancient land and the contribution to Western culture made by the original native peoples of Italy, and later Greek and Roman settlers.

Chapter 1

Naples

Naples is chilly—unusual for late March. A cold wind blows constantly from the gulf toward land. It mocks the belief that early spring in the southern Mediterranean should be warm. I have a shirt on, covered by a flimsy windbreaker that I pulled out of the pouch I found tucked in a remote pocket in my luggage. No sweater, no overcoat. It must be in the high thirties or very low forties, barely warm enough to keep the frost off the gurgling fountain across the way. White exhaust pours out from behind cars. Steam rises out of grates in the sidewalk. My glasses fog up when I walk into a warm, crowded coffee bar.

I am foolish not to have dressed more warmly. In Italy in February and March, one can wear light shirts and still break a sweat as far north as Genoa. I remain too trusting of my beliefs about delightful Italian weather, honed over more than a decade of walking in the warm Italian sun.

My first morning here I awake to look over a foreground of tall umbrella pines and see a patch of new snow on Vesuvius, which the afternoon before stood brown over the Gulf of

Naples. The giant volcano's bulk dominates everything to the east, a sword hanging over the heads of Neapolitans. Scientists warn that at any moment Vesuvius could erupt, or spawn major earthquakes, potentially killing millions. Wind whips a plume of smoke—or is it a safe cloud?—hanging above its crater. The bluster could be a *maestrale* blowing southeastward from northern France, or a dust-laden *sirocco* from the deserts of Libya.

Weather terms defeat me, just as do most new Italian words that I want to add to my inconsiderable vocabulary. Perhaps it is a function of age, of corroded synapses. I am learning Italian in my fifties. For younger people, languages appear to hold no mystery. Years ago, my then teenage daughter seemed to become fluent in French overnight. Later, she picked up basic conversational Japanese in weeks. Now, in her mid-twenties, she is just as eagerly learning Latvian. I am amazed and envious.

I must constantly refer to my well-worn, and perpetually bent, pocket dictionary, speak agonizingly slowly in restaurants, hotels, and train stations. The words do not come automatically, even after I use them many, many times.

One of the great things about Italians is that, unlike Parisians, they appreciate a foreigner's attempts at their language no matter how poor the pronunciation or syntax. The only time an Italian ever corrected my pronunciation was when I misspoke the name of his city. I used the word "Naples," a perfectly acceptable English pronunciation. A man on a train, proud to be a Neapolitan, instantly corrected me: "*è Napoli!*" he said emphatically, all the while ignoring my other mispronunciations and scattered syntax during a pleasing hour-long conversation.

Words describing weather are just as hard. I still do not understand how El Niño differs from La Niña. Italians seem to have a name for every type of breeze, every kind of storm. I only know "cold," "hot," "warm," "chilly," "breezy," and "stormy." In Italy, I vow to change, to become knowledgeable about the nuances of *il tempo* (the weather), and words that describe its subtle shifts.

Italians, even city-bred ones, appear on intimate terms with their land, and with the subtlety of how weather affects growing things and the people who cultivate them. In cities, even in the poorest quarters, potted gardens tumble their vines from window ledges packed with pots, and from balconies too narrow—or too crowded with plants—for a person to stand. Small patches along railroad tracks that in the United States would be full of wrecked cars, battered refrigerators, and rubble are cultivated, season after season, by city dwellers who spend their spring, summer, and fall weekends tilling soil and growing things.

I am sure that Italians have a name for this wind that whips through me as I huddle in the grand, open space of the Piazza del Plebiscito, cleared of automobiles in recent years by Naples' progressive mayor; and I am sure that I am cold—and regret not packing a warmer coat.

Englishman George Gissing, a Victorian writer well known among his peers, was here one hundred years ago, perhaps standing on this very corner at the southwest edge of the Plebiscito where it connects to Via C. Console and where I am looking toward the bay and at the hazy outline of the island of Capri far across the water. If the wind was whipping through him as it is me, I am sure he did not mind. There is a passage from a chapter entitled "Winter" in one of his last books—*The Private Papers of Henry Ryecroft*—that seems to capture what I perceive Gissing's attitude to be about the natural forces of weather: "For the man sound in body and serene of mind there is no such thing as bad weather; every sky has its beauty, and storms which whip the blood do but make it pulse more vigorously." Somehow this knowledge did not make me feel better as I stood there shivering. I walked quickly up to the Via Toledo, found a store with inexpensive sweaters, and bought one.

Gissing arrived in Italy on September 23, 1897, his third journey to the southern Mediterranean in nine years, and spent time in Siena working on his critical study of Charles Dickens. He completed it on November 5 and sent it to his publisher. A short time later, after a few days in Rome, he launched his famous foray into the South of Italy to rediscover the cities that originally had been founded by the Greeks.

The result of that journey, a travel narrative published in 1901, *By the Ionian Sea: Notes of a Ramble in Southern Italy*, is what drew me a century later.

His trip, so well documented in the nearly one-hundred-year-old classic, was taken after two earlier journeys to the Mediterranean, one to Rome, Florence, Venice, and Naples in 1888, and another a year later to Greece and Naples, where, according to biographer Korg, he experienced congestion of the right lung, "the first serious touch of the illness that was eventually to kill him" in 1903. Today, scholars generally believe he died of emphysema, although his death certificate is unclear about the cause.

Born in 1857 into a family of limited means, George Gissing grew into a dour man who seemed depressed much of the time and who often retreated into the recesses of his mind. He showed little outward emotion in life, took long, solitary walks in the English countryside, and acknowledged in his diary that he daydreamed about ancient Greek and Roman civilizations.

His twenty-two novels and collections of short stories dealt with English life in the Victorian Age of the late nineteenth century, and focused on the disparity among the social classes, and on life along the mean streets of the newly industrialized, smoke-belching cities.

Gissing's personal life was not a happy one. As a young man, he had been a brilliant student, particularly in the mandatory study of the classics that English schoolchildren were subjected to in that era. But he was expelled from college and briefly imprisoned after he was caught stealing from classmates to support a prostitute, with whom he had become infatuated.

In disgrace, he left England in September 1876 and eventually landed in Chicago. During this American exile, he tried his hand at teaching and later barely supported himself writing short stories of fiction for daily newspapers, including the *Chicago Tribune*. Later, he was an assistant to a traveling photographer, journeying throughout New England.

Just before his twentieth birthday in the fall of 1877, Gissing returned home, eventually marrying the prostitute he had stolen for. This was the first of two failed and, by his accounts, miserable marriages. The marriage to Marianne Helen Harrison, whom he called "Nell," caused him continual despair over her unrepentant lifestyle of alcohol and drug abuse. Through it all he continued to write. He and Nell eventually separated, but he continued to care for her through numerous health crises. In a study of Gissing's image of women, *Portraits in Charcoal*, James Haydock writes that once, when Gissing took Nell to the doctor for one of her ailments, the physician detected the presence of venereal disease. When the doctor asked her about it, she blamed her husband. Later, Gissing, who did not have the disease, told a friend that he had felt trapped during Nell's telling of her phony story to the doctor and "so endured the doctor's angry rebuke in silence."

Nell died in February 1888, just a few days after her thirtieth birthday, from the effects of untreated alcoholism and, probably, syphilis. Gissing took care of her funeral arrangements, hiring mourners, paying the mortician, clearing out her squalid room. His diary entry describing the scene in that room when he was called by Nell's landlady to identify her body is particularly compelling:

"On the door hung a poor miserable dress and a worn out ulster [a long, loose overcoat of Irish origins, made of heavy material]; under the bed was a pair of boots. Linen she had none. . . . All the money she received went in drink. . . . Her associates were women of so low a kind that even Mrs. Sherlock [the landlady] did not consider them respectable enough to visit her house. . . . I drew out the drawers. In one I found a little bit of butter and a crust of bread—most pitiful sight my eyes ever looked upon.

"She lay on the bed covered with a sheet. I looked long, long at her face, but could not recognize it . . . she had changed horribly. Her teeth all remained, white and perfect as formerly. . . . Henceforth I never cease to bear testimony against the accursed social order that brings about things of this kind. I feel that she will help me more in her death than she balked me during her life. Poor, poor thing!"

A book Gissing completed just a few months after Nell's death, *The Nether World*, was, according to his biographer Jacob Korg, "his . . . most bitter book about the problems of poverty."

Gissing scholar Maria Dimitriadou, writing in the October

The Neapolitan shellfish market flourished along via Santa Lucia in the 1880s, when the Gulf of Naples lapped at the street's edge and boats unloaded the day's catch along piers jutting into the water. Gissing saw this market during a trip to Naples in the late 1880s and reveled in the excitement and aliveness of the street.
Photo via the Internet,"Le Strade di Napoli"

1998 issue of *The Gissing Journal*, says that Gissing acknowledged "that his intellectual desire was to escape life as he knew it and dream himself into that old world, and that the names of Greece and Italy drew him as no others did and made him young again." Dimitriadou then quotes the Italian scholar Francesco Badolato's observation that Gissing's forays into Greece and Italy "provided him with the kind of refuge from the grim realities of the modern industrial and commercial world."

Gissing's third journey to the South, coming after his second marriage started breaking up and as he was continually registering serious concerns about his health, represented what he may have perceived as his final "cheery excursion," according

This was the scene that greeted Gissing in late 1897: a "wilderness of dust heaps" was filling up the area along via Santa Lucia to allow this quarter of Naples to extend several blocks into the Gulf. Gissing feared that the buildings that would be placed on this landfill would turn the Santa Lucia into an ordinary street.
Photo via the Internet, "Le Strade di Napoli"

to an editors' introduction to a memoir of a Gissing contemporary, Brian Ború Dunne. "Gissing went to Italy to escape from the most profound and extended period of depression in his life, and he came there prepared to be happy." Why not? Despite his troubled early years and disastrous second marriage, by 1895 Gissing was viewed by some literary experts as one of the three best late-Victorian-era writers, sharing company with Thomas Hardy and George Meredith. The Dunne memoir's editors say of the final Italy trip: "Gissing thus entered what is now regarded as one of the happiest periods of his life."

In November 1897, standing along the Via Santa Lucia near the Piazza del Plebiscito in Naples, Gissing looked across what was then a garbage dump-cum-landfill known today as the Santa Lucia district. That monstrous dumping of earth into the former pristine waters along that short Gulf of Naples stretch was part of a late-nineteenth-century public-works project. It extended the northwest crescent of this city hundreds of feet into the gulf. Old photographs, taken before this landfill was created, show how boats were directly tied up at a stone wall that bordered Via Santa Lucia. It was the site of the city's old shellfish market, and each day's catch was handed up from the bobbing boats to fishmongers who sold their wares on the stone embankment above.

It was a colorful, noisy place during Gissing's first and second trips in 1888 and 1889. He knew, by the time of the third trip a decade later, that this aliveness was being buried along with the tiny harbor area he witnessed being filled up with dirt and refuse.

Today on this fill, much like the one that created the Marina District of San Francisco, are six- or seven-story buildings that appear to date back to the end of the nineteenth century, when Gissing had the last unobstructed views from Via Santa Lucia of the gulf, the Sorrento Peninsula, Capri, and Ischia.

Santa Lucia is one of this struggling city's few high-rent neighborhoods. But it remains an area where people of mixed means live side by side—a typical Neapolitan lifestyle. Basement rooms in these elegant structures are occupied by entire families, and the ground-level and lower floors contain workshops, known as *officine*, and businesses of various types. The higher floors, *piani nobili*, are occupied by those who can afford the steep prices. Friends tell me this pattern is slowly shifting. As Naples becomes more Americanized, the poor and the affluent do not mix as much as they used to.

Along Via Santa Lucia are churches, cafés, restaurants, a cinema, and a take-away pizzeria. One hundred years ago Gissing had an unobstructed panorama of the gulf from this old street that used to be lined by makeshift fish-sellers' stands, replenished each morning from the boats that once were docked only a few feet away. Now the sea is three or four blocks farther south, and passersby along Via Santa Lucia get only occasional glimpses of the sea at points where newer north–south streets join at perpendicular intersections.

A Rome friend, Maria Findlow, travels to Naples several times a week to teach. In an early 1999 letter, she described an event she witnessed in Santa Lucia that shows how the old continues to mix with the new.

"I was walking along Santa Lucia during a morning of cold, windy, wet weather, and a funeral procession was winding its way towards a church. The mourners, following the coffin being pulled through the streets by a carriage being drawn by three huge, black horses, were carrying colored umbrellas contrasting with their black clothes and the black carriage.

"It is obviously the funeral of someone important—probably a *camorrista*, a local crime boss—because the ornate gold and black carriage is reserved for the rich and famous, and the police are present, including two long-haired policewomen.

"As the procession passes, men standing outside a small café make the sign of the cross, and other people come out of the shops to pay their respect to the dead. Children can be heard on the side streets shouting in Neapolitan dialect, *'Vieni, o'funnarale!'* (Come, a funeral!)."

What Gissing feared about this historic district losing much of its character as the land is unnaturally pushed out into the sea has happened. He remembered seeing a beautiful Via

Santa Lucia that, during his brief visit ten years earlier in the 1880s, offered spectacular views of the Sorrento Peninsula and Capri. Those two landmasses serve as a partial natural break-water, keeping the Gulf of Naples generally blue and serene for passersby along the little street. Now, when the panorama of Capri and the peninsula can be spied only at brief points, the view is often blocked by a screen of post–World War II industry-generated haze that settles in almost daily.

As he looked over the fill—"a wilderness of dust-heaps"—Gissing could see that the Santa Lucia would become "an ordinary street, shut in among huge houses, with no view at all."

Some things have not changed. The area above the still-cobble-stoned street was, in Gissing's time—and for centuries before—a haven for smugglers. It still is. Now, however, a police car is regularly on duty outside the offices on the seaward side of Via Santa Lucia, but bribery of police remains commonplace, and there has been a much-publicized scandal reported about this in the Italian press.

But that is hidden. Here now can be seen vegetable and fruit stalls displaying, even in winter, oranges, pineapples, tomatoes, and multicolored peppers, with garlic and red peppers hanging from the awnings. Just past a news agent's stall is the church of Santa Maria delle Catene, Our Lady of the Chains. This six-teenth-century church at one time overlooked the sea; now it overlooks modern buildings built on the hundred-year-old landfill.

Farther beyond, toward Via Partenope, which now skirts the bay at the far edge of Gissing's "dust-heap," are the fortress-like walls of Pizzofalcone, one of the city's finest old residential quarters. Via Chiatamone leads off to the north from Via Santa Lucia toward Piazza Vittoria and the Villa Comunale, a beautifully designed park used by families and courting couples.

Luxury hotels dominate the waterfront here, along the century-old landfill's edge. The city is gearing up for Italy's year 2000 Jubilee, hoping to become a "dormitory" for travelers when Rome becomes crowded with pilgrims. Via Santa Lucia ends at the waterfront, blending into a hundred-foot-long causeway over the water to the tiny island holding Castel dell'Ovo, a fortress built in the twelfth century C.E.

Something else has changed in this neighborhood. Gissing talked about the Strada di Chiaia, on the opposite side of the Piazza del Plebiscito near the uphill beginning of Via Santa Lucia. When Gissing was in the city ten years before his late 1890s visit, he remembered the strada as being boisterous and noisy with carriage drivers clamoring for passengers. It had become, by the fall of 1897, strangely quiet for reasons unknown to him. Gissing need not have worried. In early 1998, the strada, now called simply Via Chiaia, is a street with traffic roaring through at high speeds, the modern clamor replacing the old, and the street's former charm gone.

One hundred years ago, it must have been easier for Neapolitans to push into the bay rather than up the steep hills, where orange and lemon groves once released their fragrance. Now those hills behind me, known as the Vomero, are part of the city's northwest curve.

Lined with homes, multistoried apartments, shops, office buildings, and funicular stations, the slopes wait for Vesuvius to spew ash and lava, as it did in 1944, or for earthquakes to strike, like the one in 1980 that killed three thousand people, including a group of elderly who died when the poorhouse in which they were living, a once-grand eighteenth-century structure, collapsed.

In the years since, the land under the western suburb of Pozzuoli continues to rise and fall periodically, a result of seismic activity not too far below the surface. Residents have gotten used to it—a kind of fatalism that does not get in the way of life's everyday struggles.

I am staying in the Vomero, in a small, clean, inexpensive *pensione*. It serves a typical "continental" breakfast—coffee, hard roll, butter if I remember to ask for it, and various kinds of jam. I came here because friends said it would be quieter high on the hill than in the congested city below.

It requires a fifty-lira coin—roughly three cents—to take the tiny elevator to the fifth floor. The coin makes a hollow "clunk" as I drop it through the slot in the gray steel box inside. The elevator is so tight that my one bag and I completely fill the space. The car, wrapped in black metal bands, begins its ascent, suddenly jerking upwards the instant I drop the coin. After a moment it settles down and I move steadily upward toward my destination. Movie images come to mind of tiny European elevators jammed as an afterthought into stairwells in buildings built long before elevators were invented.

I had made a reservation; the *signora*, who had pushed a buzzer to unlock the giant double door on the ground floor while shouting *"Avanti!"* through the tinny speaker of the intercom, awaits me. Surprisingly, for a Neapolitan and for a woman well into her sixties, she is nearly six feet tall. She is brusque, and her English is as imperfect as my Italian,

She says my last name, horribly mispronouncing it, as do most Americans. I nod and she turns on her heel, saying something that sounds like "Go with me," and leads me, scurrying to keep up, into the lobby. I want a room with a view. After all, we are on a mountainside high above one of the most beautiful gulfs in the world.

"*Con vista?*" I ask hopefully when she quotes me the surprisingly low daily rate. "A view?" she asks incredulously. "Look all around," she says. "All buildings everywhere." Then she smiles. "All rooms the same. And clean and warm."

I give her my passport so she can record my vital statistics on the forms that all Italian innkeepers must use to log in their guests. She hands me a map of the city. "Return please, when finished," she says. The map is glossy, full of creases. Points of interest are circled in many different colors of ink. Some street names are smudged into oblivion. Obviously it has been well used. I seem to be holding the community map.

Her words are short, direct. She is all business. But when she smiles I feel her Italian warmth. I like this place and decide I like her.

She leads me to my room, pointing out the shower—"Please. Only one shower each day," she commands—and other facilities en route. She points into a small room with a handful of small, round tables and light-green-checked tablecloths. "For breakfast," she says. "You may have, if you hurry."

I turn to deposit my bag quickly in the large, sunny room overlooking the street leading to the funicular station whose slow-moving car brought me up to the Vomero from the frenzied Neapolitan street a mile or so below. I walk back into the hallway to get my breakfast and almost bump into a wheelchair holding an older woman, dressed in black and wearing a white shawl around her shoulders. I nod and say loudly, perhaps too loudly, "*Buon giorno!*" The old woman nods imperceptibly.

"*Mia madre,*" says my hostess quietly, her face softening as she looks at her mother sitting there. "We hope you do not make noise. Her room is here, next to you. We care for her. This is her house."

Gissing had set out from the harbor below, in a small coastal steamer, in the late fall of 1897 to begin his journey into Magna Graecia. Latin for Great Greece, the name encompasses the part of southern Italy where the ancient Greeks from across the Adriatic founded magnificent cities and temples dedicated to the gods. This was centuries before the native peoples of central Italy, living in tiny wooden and mud huts on the Palatine Hill next to the Tiber River, evolved into the Roman Republic and later the Roman Empire.

Most books on the history of Italy begin with the Romans. A few might dedicate a sentence or two acknowledging the peninsula's prehistoric Bronze Age and Iron Age tribes, or the colonizing Greeks who first brought what today is recognized as modern-style democracy, and Western art and culture, to this then remote, fertile land.

The Greek cities these colonials established, which one hundred years ago Gissing sought to rediscover, rimmed the sole of Italy's boot. Many others spread northward, along the west coast to a point near the ankle. In Italy, Greece's oldest and northernmost settlements were on what is now the island of Ischia, at nearby Cumae and, where I am standing now, Neapolis. Greece also had colonies in Sicily and in even more distant locations such as southern France.

In his journey ten decades ago, Gissing missed some of the more remote Greek centers—then still-buried cities that had to wait until the twentieth century to be uncovered by archaeologists. The precise locations of others recorded in ancient writings still have not been found.

The *Encyclopedia Britannica* sheds some light. Cumae, founded in the mid-eighth century B.C.E.—about 740—is believed to be the oldest Greek colony on the southern Italian mainland. The one on the island of Ischia was slightly earlier, perhaps the first in Italy. More than three hundred years later, Cumae was overwhelmed by Italic tribes, who inserted their own culture and language into the daily community life. Republican Rome, moving to expand its grip beyond the Tiber, conquered the city one hundred years later, in the mid-fourth century B.C.E., and Cumae became a quiet country town, ultimately vanishing in the Middle Ages. In modern times there is nearby Cuma, whose name alludes to the vanished city's original Greek appellation.

Neapolis was luckier. It was founded one hundred fifty years after Cumae, probably as an extension of that and other colonies. But unlike Cumae after its subjugation, Romans, enamored of Greek culture, allowed Hellenic Neapolitans to preserve their language for nearly one thousand years, well after C.E. 400. The term *Hellenic* refers to the flowering of Greek culture, art, and philosophy roughly from the time of Alexander the Great to Julius Caesar in Rome, or 336–31 B.C.E. The Roman elite built palaces around the temperate Gulf of Naples and used this Greek center as a pleasure resort.

In 1897, Gissing was only interested in visiting southern Italy's known Greek centers. For his one-month trip in November–December 1897, he left out of his itinerary the colonies that extended into Sicily and into the south of France. He was familiar with colonies in Sicily and later lived in France, but he never wrote specifically about them.

I am here to follow the path Gissing laid out in his classic travel narrative *By the Ionian Sea—Notes on a Ramble in Southern Italy*, first published in 1901, just two years before he died, and in print almost continually since.

Chapter 2

A Hand in the Pocket

I had arrived in Naples a day earlier. Walking off the Rome train into the city's heart, I carried preconceived notions that this strange and beautiful city—built over idyllic, ancient Neapolis—was dangerous. My concern, I soon discovered, was well founded.

Naples, with its purse snatchers and pickpockets, can be as unsettling as the guidebooks warn, especially to tourists who foolishly dangle cameras and bags off of shoulders, or stuff credit cards and cash into pockets.

But Naples, with its sights, sounds, and smells, is fabulously ambrosial as well. Outdoor markets are everywhere. At the fish-sellers', swordfish heads sit on beds of ice, dull, filmy eyes peering upwards, spikes pointing to the sky. Octopus and squid, gathered in that day's misty pre-dawn, lie in tangled heaps. Mackerel, sardines, and all types of shellfish pepper the slippery, ice-encrusted tabletops.

Elsewhere in these markets that seem to spring up spontaneously from one neighborhood to the next, heaps of tomatoes, peppers of all shapes and sizes and shades, tumble out of turned-over baskets, alongside several different kinds of lettuce and other green, leafy things I have never seen before. I ask the names, am told, and then, overwhelmed, promptly forget the just-proffered words.

People are talking with, gesticulating at, touching, one another. Naples is alive—despite the apparent poorness of its many quarters.

Still I am nagged by the potential of danger to the unwary. I try to be aware of where I am or whether I am being watched, frustrated that I cannot completely relax. I remind myself that if this were Los Angeles or New York City—two cities I would not hesitate to visit—I could be blown away by a mugger intent on getting the few dollars in my pocket. Here, guide-books and friends have told me, such sudden and direct violence is rare, especially against tourists. But if you let down your guard in crowded buses or on narrow, jammed streets, you might feel a tug at your shoulder bag or, more likely, never even realize your pocket has been picked until long after you have stepped off the bus and it slowly dawns on you that, somehow, you feel lighter.

I have learned that, unlike American muggers, most Italian thieves steal in like cats and tiptoe out again. Fortunately, the law-abiding citizens—most of the people—with their joy of life, basic "Italian-ness," more than make up for a thief's callousness.

I discovered both the good and the bad during my journey that I began in early 1998, a few months past the centenary of Gissing's departure from Naples for the cities of Magna Graecia.

Gissing, by all contemporary accounts, was a dour man. He found little about 1890s southern Italy to praise; his joy was confined to daydreaming about life in the time of the Greek colonists. He voiced numerous laments that today, against the backdrop of modern Italy, seem silly. The worst Gissing could say in print about Naples was that the Neapolitan organ-grinders he had first heard during brief visits in the late 1880s had disappeared because of police intervention. And that the city seemed to be growing in an awkward, nonclassical way.

If only my modern reality were that simple!

I did not know I was twenty dollars lighter until seconds after stepping off a trolley near the port. The crowded trolley had wound its way along the foot of the city where it rims the Gulf of Naples. The setting was picturesque, intoxicating—the stuff of postcards. I was heading to the port to find out if there was a boat that could take me south to Paola. After Naples, Paola was Gissing's first stop along the Tyrrhenian coast. The tiny village, perched on the slope of the coastal mountains, was, in the days before extensive railroads and north–south freeways, the logical place to begin the narrow, twisty climb by carriage over an ancient road into interior Calabria and Gissing's first major stop, Cosenza.

In reconstructing events of my unnerving encounter aboard that tram, I remember someone's knee bumping into my leg. I must have written it off to the fact that I was standing on a crowded trolley, and, frankly, I was mesmerized by the sounds, feel, and smells of the place. We passengers were bunched at the middle exit, waiting for our stops. I climbed off at the port, still unaware of what had just happened. A few steps later, it sank in. I reached into my pocket, already knowing what I would not find there.

I glanced back at the tram, disappearing in the light haze ahead—relieved that my credit cards and other cash were hidden elsewhere. The twenty dollars or so in lire wasn't important. The money clip, a souvenir from Mexico, was. I muttered evil thoughts as I turned and continued walking to the port ticket office.

I knew there was a train to Paola, but had hoped to get there as Gissing did, aboard a small coastal boat. *"Niente, signore!"* Nothing. Boats to Capri, yes. To Messina or Palermo in Sicily, yes. To Paola, no. *"Il treno, signore,"* the ticket seller said, pointing behind me toward the city and in the general direction of the *stazione centrale.*

I nodded, turned, and began a long walk into the heart of the old city. I had had enough of crowded trams for a while. My adventures with Italy's darker side, finally catching up with me, were not over. I still had lessons to learn.

On a narrow, crowded street—my guidebook said it originally was laid out by the Greeks—a burly young man with dark, curly hair hanging in shiny ringlets around his shoulders slipped up behind me as I waited with other pedestrians for a small delivery truck to back out of our path.

Once again lost in thought, probably imagining what this constricted street might have looked like two thousand five hundred years earlier, I was pulled backwards by a sharp tug on my small shoulder bag, which contained my notebook, guide-book, and map. The young man yanked several times. Barely holding on to my balance, I pulled back, swinging out my leg and catching him with my toe on the side of his leg, just above his knee. He let go and ran into a side street, jumping over, and disappearing behind, an orange construction barrier.

Shaken—and, despite all the warnings I had read, stunned by such un-Italian direct confrontation—I hurriedly walked away, clutching the bag containing my irreplaceable notebook. In mid-stride, I felt a tap on my shoulder. A middle-aged woman who had seen what happened told me in hurried, breathless Italian that I must keep my bag between my body and the building, not toward the street. She smiled and patted my shoulder. I muttered thanks and moved away.

Moments later, a young woman, a *ragazza*, who appeared to be a student and who had her leather backpack twisted around to her front, both arms through the straps, stopped me. She, too, had witnessed the assault and had run after me.

"*Napoli* is very, very dangerous," she told me in perfect English but still using the Italian pronunciation of her city's name. She figured me to be exactly what I was: an American tourist. "You must always watch your bag and keep it at your side, toward the building," she said, repeating the older woman's admonition and the advice I had read a dozen times in guidebooks.

"I am so very sorry and I apologize for my beautiful city," she said, looking almost tearful. "And you appear injured." She pointed to my hand, which was dripping blood from the cuticle of my little finger. "Here." She grabbed my arm and led me into a *farmacia* (pharmacy), a few feet away. She asked the clerk inside for some tape, explaining in rapid Italian what had happened.

The young clerk ripped the small bandage from its wrapper and pulled it tightly around my finger as I stood there numbly, feeling light-headed and probably in mild shock.

I asked the clerk how much. "*Niente,*" nothing, she said. Then, in a level voice that sounded more like a warning than a passing farewell, the clerk said, "*Buona fortuna, signore.*"

Outside, the young woman continued: "There are few jobs here and some of the young people use desperate means. I am so sorry." I thanked her profusely. She smiled, then turned and walked away, clutching her "backpack" tightly to her chest.

I looked for a quiet place—a church perhaps, or a tree-lined park—where I could relax, unwind, and contemplate the events of the last few minutes. I ambled along, careful to keep my bag between me and buildings, and marveling at the kindness of strangers. They, not petty thieves, are who I choose to remember when I think of my brief time in Naples.

Chapter 3

Tales of the Conquerors

I long to linger in Naples. I know there must be redeeming qualities under the grime of this crumbling, congested city. One of the best descriptions I have read of this place and its modern challenges is in *Midnight in Sicily*, by Australian Peter Robb. He wrote that Stendhal described Naples in 1817 as "the most beautiful city in the universe." Stendhal and Goethe each called it one of the three great capitals of Europe, alongside London and Paris. This is hard to believe today.

The city's role in Europe changed when Italy was unified in 1861. Vittorio Emanuele II, the king of Sardinia, became the king of a united Italy. By 1861 the Spanish Bourbons had lost their influence and Naples became a provincial capital. By 1870, the new nation's political machinery had been moved to Rome.

This unification process followed after Giuseppe Garibaldi, born in Nice before that Italian city was part of France, led an expedition to liberate the South from the Bourbons, who had been given sway here by Austria decades earlier. Historians still debate Garibaldi's motives, but when he heard of an anti-Bourbon revolt in Palermo, he decided it was time to conquer Sicily, long held by the Neapolitan Bourbons. Without much support from the government in the North, he recruited the famous "Thousand," actually, according to one source, 1,087 men who largely were northern Italians and nearly all students, young professional men, and artisans. Only about one hundred of these "red shirts," so called because of the uniforms they wore, were southerners.

These volunteers sailed from Genoa, landed in Sicily in May 1860, and, with rusty muskets and bayonets, took the island in the name of Vittorio Emanuele within two months. The Sicilians supported them, but started taking matters into their own hands. Garibaldi had to suppress a series of peasant revolts before he could set his sights on liberating Naples—and all the South—from the Bourbons in the name of the northern Italian king.

In August 1860, Garibaldi, fortified by thousands of new volunteers, crossed the Strait of Messina and easily won a series of skirmishes against the Bourbons on the mainland. Three weeks after landing, he took Naples. Neapolitans welcomed Garibaldi as a hero because they did not like the Bourbons. The city's largest square, in front of the main train station and now choked with cars and buses, is named for him, as are many main squares throughout Italy. But the Neapolitans were not enthusiastic about being part of a united Italy; they gave the king a lukewarm reception later that year.

This ambivalence of the early Neapolitans is characterized by their reaction when Rome became the nation's capital in 1870 after it had been wrested from the pope. Naples' leaders changed the name of a main boulevard from the Spanish appellation of Via Toledo to Via Roma. People in that section of the city simply refused to use the new name. The old name, Via Toledo, now is back in favor, and contrary Neapolitans still often refer to the street as Via Roma, despite what the street signs and official maps say. It is typically Italian that they see no confusion in this juxtaposition that does much to confuse the casual visitor.

So, in the 1860s and the immediate decades after, Naples and southern Italy played virtually no role in the unification process. The South was simply invaded once again, this time by idealistic northern liberals, and then turned over to "northerners who never wanted to rule the South, and who certainly had not fought for it," according to Martin Clark, author of *The Italian Risorgimento*. The North "acquired it not because the Neapolitans themselves wanted that outcome, nor because of any feat of arms by the [northern] army, but because a great guerrilla leader and military genius [Garibaldi] so decides."

And Naples over the decades lingered on, devolving into a third-world city filled with squalor and besieged by cholera well past the middle of the twentieth century. In the early 1970s, Robb tells us, nearly half of Neapolitan houses lacked bathing facilities, and only one-fifth had indoor toilets.

The city today is fighting back, say my Italian and expatriate friends—some of whom still refuse to come here. But I wonder if the struggle is overwhelming. The Neapolitan crime organization, the *camorra*, is growing. Young people, like the *ragazzo* who yanked at my bag and picked my pocket, have few employment options. Meanwhile, as in troubled American cities, televisions blast messages of prosperity and images of material wealth into the crowded, shabby homes in

Naples' desperate center, showing the people how the rest of the world—and especially northern Italy—lives.

There is prosperity "everywhere but in the South," a young man told me during a brief, but revealing, conversation at a bus stop.

Modern Italy has another danger as well: the automobile. It is distressing most everywhere along the peninsula, and in Naples, particularly so. Narrow, Neapolitan streets follow the course of Roman and, before them, Greek, roadways. In modern times, many of these streets remain only wide enough for two passing chariots. Yet, much of the day, they are jammed by honking cars and smoking buses, or are torn up for resurfacing. Roads remain under construction for months, even years, with utility lines exposed and few walkways provided for pedestrians, who regularly navigate rubble, loose cobblestones, open pits, piles of dirt, and cars parked on sidewalks.

Much of the street work during my visit in early 1998 was along the busy Via Toledo—or, depending on one's politics, Via Roma—the major artery designed and built under the Spanish viceroy Don Pedro de Toledo in 1536.

I walked past one spot on the Via Toledo/Via Roma where drainpipes from under a building were dripping evil-looking liquid into a hole dug near the edge of the torn-up street. A disconnected sewer line waiting to be reconnected? How long it had been like this, uncovered, uncapped, I had no idea. There were no workers in sight. Perhaps it would be untended for days, weeks.

It was a strange contrast: many people wearing stylish coats, furs and leathers, pushing past me on the narrow, temporary sidewalk, a few feet from an open sewer line, in front of stores hawking the latest fashions. Mysteriously, in a city rampant with poverty, the stylish stores seem to survive, and the people generally appear healthy and well fed.

Here, across busy streets, pedestrians do not have the right of way. They must pick their openings, looking left and right, arms tucked in, holding possessions close like a footballer heading for a score. Traffic lights and Walk lights, only colorful window dressing in this troubled and crowded city, are ignored.

My distress over jammed streets, open sewers, and what appeared to my American sensibilities to be abject poverty all contrasted sharply with Englishman Gissing's now ludicrous 1897 lament that organ-grinders had disappeared. His consternation had even carried over to Paola, my destination the following day. There, he bemoaned in the late 1890s that rural Italians were not wearing their traditional garb—their colorful costumes that painted such an idyllic, stereotypic picture in his mind.

Eventually, I guess, we are all doomed to watch our stereotypes and preconceptions crumble. The movement away from traditional peasant dress, Gissing believed, was the result of "this destroying age" of nineteenth-century modernization. Strong words, but, in view of his Victorian, pre-automobile sensibility, he believed they were appropriate.

Those words are appropriately strong today, if not more so. If only Gissing had lived to see the impact of the automobile on Italian cities! From my standpoint in the 1990s, "this destroying age" is best represented by the vehicles that pack narrow Italian streets from north to south. Another British novelist writing one hundred years after Gissing, Ian McEwan, uses in his book *Amsterdam* the most appropriate phrase: "tyranny of traffic."

Professor Baldassare Conticello, one of Italy's preemi-
nent archaeologists and
an expert in early Greek
colonization in southern
Italy, checks a reference
from one of the hundreds
of books in his Rome apartment library.
Photo by John Keahey

I certainly can accept that it is not the job of modern Italians
to walk around in "peasant dress" to satisfy the Gissings of the
tourist world. Change, after all, is inevitable and proper. But I
do regret the loss of serenity that I imagine used to hang over
once quiet town squares that today have become giant parking
lots. I grieve at my inability to walk down a narrow street lined
with magnificent medieval buildings crafted out of stones pil-
laged from ancient Greek and Roman monuments without
being narrowly missed by small, darting cars or by careening
teenagers on high-pitched, whining motor scooters.

Of course, while lost in such idyllic thoughts I choose to
ignore why southern Italians, late last century and early this
century, fled what today's tourists view as quaint villages and
countryside, vowing never to return or to look back at the

crushing, bone-jarring poverty, malaria, and near starvation that were so prevalent here then and that still have not entirely disappeared.

"You cannot eat 'quaint,'" said an Italian man with whom I shared a train compartment a few days later as he shook out the newspaper he held, buried his nose deep within its pages, and silence enveloped our small, southbound compartment.

Within this quiet space—the only sounds being a rustle of the gentleman's newspaper and the clack of wheels—I shifted from reflecting about Italian poverty to the question of why Greece moved west so long ago.

I recalled a conversation in Rome, in a small, cramped, book-lined study located in an exquisite apartment owned by one of Italy's leading archaeologists, Professor Baldassare Conticello. We have an appointment for an early afternoon lunch. I am delayed at the airport, picking up a friend who is being treated at a first-aid station for what could be food poisoning acquired during his long flight from Texas. I call the professor, and we reschedule for dinner. My friend is deposited in his room, sleeping off the mysterious affliction, which was never resolved. I arrive at the professor's home at five o'clock and leave around midnight, my stomach full of fine Italian food prepared by Signora Lucia Conticello, my head full of ancient history.

Conticello has an impressive résumé. He has been superintendent of archaeology for many regional areas, including ten years at Pompeii. Nearing retirement, the sixty-seven-year-old scholar is central inspector for archaeology in the Italian Ministry for Cultural Goods and Environment.

As I write this, I visualize the mustachioed professor at his desk. Behind him are floor-to-ceiling bookshelves taking up most of the tiny room. Sometimes, to underscore a point, he reaches across the desk to where I am writing in my notebook, the index finger of his right hand tapping the back of my hand.

Frequently, he jumps from his chair, scans his bookshelves, and pulls down and opens a volume to illustrate a detail. He is passionate, but calmly so. When my passion over the subject matter rises, I gesture expansively, raise my voice, and struggle with the words, whether Italian or English. Years of digging into the ancient past have made Conticello reflective. He leaves the outward display of emotion to students—and interviewers.

His appearance is conservative. He is wearing a comfortable forest green sweater covering a pale blue shirt cinched together at the neck by a darker blue tie, specked with reds and yellows, that peeks above the sweater's collar. He says he purchased most of his shirts at Brooks Brothers in New York City, a place he loves to visit.

He fits my image of a scholar, pausing occasionally to rub his eyes with long, tapered fingers that look like a piano player's rather than those of someone who has pulled artifacts from historic rubble or unearthed massive Roman and Greek columns and statues. All that is missing to complete the professorial image is a pipe or wire-rimmed spectacles. He does not smoke or drink alcohol. *"Sono astemio,"* he says with a sigh.

He used to smoke cigars— "the ones called *toscani*, a typical Italian cigar made of Kentucky and Burley tobaccos"—until late 1998.

"I was famous among my friends for always having a cigar in my mouth. All my official and private photos are with a cigar. Finally, my family and my friends convinced me to renounce. I did it many times in my life; once for three years. I hope that this is the right one."

But why no wine? I asked.

That, too, is unfortunate, he told me, sighing.

"I used to drink wine and I make my own wine: *vigna d'Aglian-ico* from Rionero in Vulture, Potenza. Recently we discovered I have a C hepatitis still going on and I was forced to surrender." He offers me wine, from his private label, at dinner, but alas I, too, for reasons of health, must say, *"Anch'io"*—Me too—*"Sono astemio."*

"Ah. *Ho capito. Bravo,*" I understand. Good for you, he says wistfully and, for both of us, sadly.

We move from the pleasures of the flesh to those of the soul.

Conticello lectures to his solitary visitor as if to a class, but in a way that captivates, holds attention. His words paint vivid, exciting pictures. Tough concepts, despite his heavily accented English, turn from murky to clear.

The Greeks, the professor tells me, are behind much of Rome's cultural greatness. Greeks captured by the Romans, he says, built the Latin language for their jailers in the third century B.C.E. The Romans did not use abstract expressions in their speech before the influence of Greeks. "This is a pencil," Romans could say in Latin. What they could not put into words is the concept behind the pencil. The Greeks changed that.

What drove their much earlier expansion into Magna Grae-cia, then wide open to sophisticated colonists? Frustrated Greek merchants, the professor tells me. Ah, I say to myself. Once again, money *is* power.

He explains: In ancient Egypt, the people believed the king was the gods' representative on earth. He owned everything: the land, the army, the people. The Greeks never took it this far. For them, the earth was legally the property of a single people, but mostly the king's and the aristocrats'. But sometimes, Conticello says, private individuals—and even, on occasion, Greek peasants—owned property.

Meanwhile, religion, a concept long used by governments to instill fear and keep diverse populations under control, was inseparable from the State. Such a combination of religion and state slows progress and hinders change, Conticello believes.

Eventually, frustrated Greek merchants sailed the Mediterranean world, buying spices and selling vases. Between 900 and the end of 800 B.C.E., Greek cities and towns faced economic uncertainty. Social rebellions abounded. There were numerous conflicts among landowners and merchants, seafarers, and the more affluent classes. Greek merchants made lots of money, but had little power.

This forced the most bold, courageous, and enterprising among them to migrate east and west. Away from mainland Greece, they established a new form of State, based on a larger, and more democratic, distribution of power.

Conticello pauses. Knowing that my college background decades earlier focused on U.S. history, he smiles and says, "There is in this a similarity with the Pilgrims leaving for the New World of North America."

Southern Italy, including Sicily, was one of the Greeks' destinations, and the western coast of modern Turkey another. The towns these Greek merchants founded in Magna Graecia, the name given the western colonies, flourished. At one time, Syrakusai, modern Siracusa in southeastern Sicily, was wealthier than Athens, located on the mainland of Greece. Syrakusai also became stronger, defeating Athens in several key battles on Sicilian soil.

Eventually, in the sixth century B.C.E., the merchants got

wealthier, raised armies, and returned to Greece, importing their new form of democratic government, principally to Athens. They started with the election of a *tyran*, a ruler for life, but quickly evolved toward elections of rulers and other authorities who served limited terms.

"So there you have it," the professor says. He sums up the evening's lesson: "In the sixth century B.C.E. was born in Greece the main institutions of modern democracy: the splitting of powers among three branches of government—the rulers, the lawmaking body, the courts—creation of a national army where all male citizens could participate rather than just the aristocracy, and the idea of 'one man, one vote.' "

Here also was the development of the Greek temple, as the center of religion, distinctly separate from the State.

Under this earliest form of democracy, Greece flourished. Before his death in 323 B.C.E., Alexander the Great had launched what is known as the Hellenistic era—a time of philosophers and magnificent strides in arts. That era lasted until after 31 B.C.E., approximately the historical time of Christ's birth and when Rome's first emperor, Augustus, was in power.

Alexander's Greek world had become divided into a series of monarchies, ruled by Alexander's heirs. This lack of cohesiveness would lead to the Roman subjugation, first of the Greeks in Italy and then of the peoples on mainland Greece.

This dynamic Greek culture was absorbed centuries later by the Romans and became the foundation of Western society.

So why didn't the Greeks survive as a major power in the then known ancient world conquered by the greatest Greek of all, Alexander the Great? How did Rome emerge, conquer all of Italy, and blend the southern Italian Greeks so smoothly into Roman society?

The answer really is simple, Conticello says. The Greeks continued to fight among themselves, city against city, and were never unified as a nation. "They were so sophisticated philosophically and so well trained in the arts—so inward looking—that they never understood that the fighting among themselves kept them from being a great power."

They were just a collection of little towns, each with a little power. Conversely, the Romans, after consolidating power among Rome's seven hills and varied tribes, became unified.

Here the professor smiles ironically.

"The Romans were shepherds who went down from the Palatine [one of Rome's original seven hills] with the idea of conquering the world. The Greeks never thought that way."

Nor do, it seems, modern-day Italians, who, Conticello says, in the wake of the fall of Fascism in 1945, are content to let others do the job of policing the world. "The United States does a fine job of this for us," he says, referring to the Gulf War, Bosnia, Kosovo.

Then he explains: "We Italians *are not* the heirs of the Romans, as the Fascists [and Mussolini] thought. We, as a people, never took from the Romans this concept of ruling the entire world. After the fall of the Roman (Western) Empire and the invasion of the land by the [Goths], we lost forever the good taste of freedom being subjected to, and subjugated by, wave after wave of invaders."

Once Rome fell, the economic power moved from the Italian peninsula to the periphery of the former Empire: France, Spain, and North Africa. When the empire was divided into two parts, about half a millennium following Christ's birth, the power, Conticello says, passed to Germany in the West and to Byzantium, or Constantinople, in the East.

"As the Greeks did, in Roman times we built magnificent monuments; we developed splendid forms of art; we created high, intellectual thoughts. We became cultural *giants*—and political *dwarfs!*"

Chapter 4

A Sicilian in Naples

The train roared southwest out of Naples' *stazione centrale*. I settled in, sharing my compartment with an aging Neapolitan
businessman who was headed for Sicily to spend Easter, still a
few weeks away, with his widowed mother. I didn't ask his
age—or hers—but he must have been in his early seventies. He
sat, thin and erect, almost regal, already in place when I
entered the compartment. He never stood in the two or so
hours we were together, but I suspected that if he did, he would
be tall, well over six feet. Most southern Italians, particularly
Sicilians, are short, stocky.

This gentleman had a fine goatee, clipped tightly against his
chin and well groomed. A clump of white hair framed his face
like a well-combed mane, cresting his long, gently sloping
forehead above a distinguished nose that sloped quickly down-
ward at the same angle as his brow. He was impeccably dressed
in a light-chocolate suit and a creamy tan shirt, set off with a
custard-yellow tie and complete with cuffs held closed by

gold-colored links. On the seat next to him lay an expensive-looking overcoat of a lighter brown.

I could picture this man, walking arm and arm with a male companion, down a narrow Neapolitan or Sicilian street, speaking low into his friend's ear, gesturing with his free hand, his coat slung over his shoulders, arms out of the sleeves, like a cape—like so many inspired gentlemen of regal bearing I have seen all over Italy. Linking arms with a companion of the same gender is common in Italy. I have seen it between small children, teenagers, adults, and the elderly. They hold close together and bend toward one another to speak in low tones, twisting their head toward the other's ear and making eye contact as often as possible.

This *signore* had been a bookseller, he said with obvious pride, a dealer in both new and rare volumes. I could visualize his long, tapered fingers lovingly caressing the well-worn pages of dusty books. He wore half-spectacles, the kind used only for reading. The glasses sat low on his nose; he looked over the tops as he spoke to me.

We talked for about half an hour in an interesting combination of English and Italian phrases, each struggling to communicate with the other. I was asking him about the economic conditions in the Mezzogiorno, a name Italians use to mean either "midday" or "noon," or to describe Italy's southern half, which encompasses the regions of Abruzzi, Molise, Campania (the region that includes Naples), Puglia, Basilicata, and Calabria. It also includes the islands of Sicily and Sardinia. A writer friend tells me that the reference alludes to the noonday sun, the hottest of the day. The South is known for the sun's burning, inescapable intensity during the long Mediterranean summer.

The gentleman on the southbound train told me that as a middle-class American, I could have no comprehension of what it is like in the South. Our communication soon ended. Neither of us could pursue the nuances of the other's language. I ran out of Italian words; he ran out of English phrases. For the remainder of my few hours' ride down the Tyrrhenian coast to Páola, we sat in comfortable silence—he buried in a newspaper, me with my eyes on the rolling scenery of the west coast of the Italian boot.

My thoughts were a mix of archaeology and poverty. I knew the train's tracks were crossing over the buried remains of ancient coastal trading cities used by Greeks and Romans alike, their precise locations lost centuries ago under the rubble left by vast armies: Saracens, Germans, Normans, Spaniards, the French. Some came only once; others returned again and again. Archaeologists know those cities are there somewhere. Buried under modern towns and villages, no doubt. Or under alluvial deposits washed down by streams and rivers flowing west and south out of Calabria.

Many times during this trip I would spend long moments trying to understand the sad economics of the South and why it differs so much from the North. The old man sitting across from me had tried to describe it, but our language barrier proved insurmountable.

What truly made clear to me the plight of "the other Italy" was a careful reading of the classic memoir by Carlo Levi, who, following World War II, wrote *Christ Stopped at Eboli*. Despite the title, the book does not suggest that Christ actually visited that small town in Campania. Instead, in the manner of speech used by peasants of the period, Levi tells us, Christianity stopped there, failing to spread into the darker, more mountainous inland reaches of Calabria and Basilicata.

To southern Italians, Levi wrote, "Christian" means "human being." And the poor people of the South were saying: "We're not Christians, we're not human beings; we're not thought of as men but simply as beasts, beasts of burden, or even less than beasts, mere creatures of the wild." The people of the South, at least before World War II under Fascism and, for centuries before under a succession of conquerors, "live in a world of their own." It is their inward protection from centuries of dealing with forces beyond their control.

Levi's book is about his year-long forced exile in the mid-1930s. He, a northern Italian writer and outspoken anti-Fascist, spent the time deep in the mountains of Lucania, now known as Basilicata, a province in the heart of the boot's mountainous interior. The region's name, for centuries, had been Basilicata. But Mussolini, in his quest to create a new twentieth-century Roman empire, gave the region the old Roman name, Lucania. After Mussolini's fall, Lucania once again became Basilicata.

Levi described, in vivid detail, the conditions endured by the southern peasants from the time their land was first affected by Phoenician traders from Troy more than three thousand years ago. These traders first introduced a "set of values diametrically opposed to those of the ancient peasant civilization. The Phoenicians brought religion and the State, and the religion of the State. . . . The invaders brought also arms and an army, escutcheons, heraldry, and war. Their religion was a violent one, demanding human sacrifice. . . . The ancient Italians, meanwhile, lived on the land, knowing neither sacrifice nor religion."

This kind of conquering and the repeated subjugation of

In the mountains just inland from Italy's west coast between Sapri and
Paola, two Calabrians meet along a narrow, two-lane roadway in the midst
of an olive orchard. The man on the left is carrying a piece of olive wood
he just cut from one of his decades-, if not centuries-, old trees that dot this
southern Mediterranean land. *Photo by John Keahey*

these southerners happened century after century, as foreign
invaders and Rome itself swept over the land. The southern
Italians from earliest, almost mythological, times have been
leery of the State, viewing it always as something imposed on
them rather than something they were part of. Instead, they
prefer loyalty to family, village, and province above all else.

For example, more than two thousand years ago, many of
these peoples rebelled against the yoke of Rome, even going so
far as to ally themselves with Carthage in North Africa—from
whom they had as much to fear as from the Romans—to help
them toss off Roman control.

Levi tells us that the period of the Italic wars between native tribes and the expanding Romans gave Rome much difficulty. In the end, the southerners failed to evade the more powerful and unified Roman State. Levi says, "But they kept their individuality and did not mingle [as did other conquered peoples all over the Mediterranean world eager for coveted Roman citizenship] with their conquerors."

No one, in the South's long history, ever tried to make the people independent. The Normans ruled here between C.E. 1130 and 1198, and were succeeded by the Germans. Then came the French in 1266, who greatly expanded the power of feudal nobility. The peasants were then taken over and taxed heavily by the Aragonese, an independent kingdom in what is now northeast Spain, bordering on France. These late-Middle-Ages rulers required payments on sheep and other livestock. It obviously was in their best interests that livestock herds be expanded, so the rulers worked to reduce the number of small farmers and agricultural laborers, and converted cropland to pasture.

Eventually, in 1734, southern Italy and Sicily became an independent Kingdom of Naples under the Spanish Bourbons, but the Mezzogiorno continued to be dominated by feudal landowners well beyond Italy's unification in 1861, when the Bourbons were driven out by Italians from the North led by Garibaldi.

It took World War II and subsequent land reform to eliminate the peasant class that Levi found in the Fascist 1930s. But in many updated encyclopedias, the Mezzogiorno still is defined as the "economically underdeveloped region" of southern Italy. Such baggage!

.   .   .

Even in modern times, the South's poor chafe against Rome. The government, with its ability to tax and conscript, simply is not trusted. As late as the 1930s, the southerners had a different concept of what was and was not lawful, compared to the Fascist State's view. The laws decreed from Rome can well be ignored, southerners believed; the laws of reason and good sense, Levi tells us, were followed instead. "A man is 'lawful' if he behaves as he should; a wine is 'lawful' if it is not watered." A petition signed by members of the pre–World War II peasant class was viewed by them as "lawful," but not by the Fascist State, which would toss the signers into jail. The laws of the State made no sense to the southerners' sense of reasoning, which was honed during centuries of subjugation.

"Just as long as Rome controls our local affairs and wields the power of life and death over us we shall go on like dumb animals," Levi quotes one frustrated southerner objecting to a Fascist demand.

Levi, a physician by training, recounts how the pre–World War II Fascist government did not want him treating patients during his year-long exile to the South, even when the sick peasants in their remote villages had nowhere else to turn for medical help. One man died because Fascist bureaucrats would not allow Levi to see him, and villagers grumbled that Rome poured millions into its war to conquer Abyssinia (modern-day Ethiopia) but refused to send money to control the malaria that had for centuries ravaged the southern Italian peasants.

Italian friends have explained to me their distrust of the Italian State, even in today's more sociable, humanistic times.

"When we pay money to the State, we know it is wasted on giant projects that never get finished," says one who defends why Italians are famous for dodging income-tax obligations.

"At best, our money is lost; at worst stolen. Why should we?"

I have often wondered whether there was ever a peaceful period in the Mezzogiorno. Did one or two consecutive generations ever live out placid lives between periods of conquest and subjugation, decade after decade, century after century? There must have been such periods, but historians tend to focus more on radical changes that involve hardship, mass death, and destruction, than on periods of blissful calm, if any ever existed here.

Chapter 5

No Boats Stop at Paola

Paola *stazione* came into view. The train stopped briefly. I said good-bye to the elderly Sicilian; he smiled warmly and nodded, and I jumped out, bag in hand, at the bottom of a hill that one hundred years ago likely was barren of buildings, including this train station, which must have been built after Gissing's visit; hence his reliance on the coastal steamer. It was mid-morning—a bit later in the day than when Gissing climbed off the small ship from Naples. I asked a train worker if any boats called here now. "Never," he said. "This is not a port." He looked slightly amused at my question.

I had covered the distance from Naples in a few hours; it took Gissing a night of steaming. I would have preferred his way, but then I would not have met the *signore* going to Sicily to visit his mother.

Gissing saw a tiny, "yellowish little town" set high against the coastal mountains that shield inland Calabria from the outside world. There is less yellow among the buildings today. Perhaps there is just a hint of that fine intensity that matches the color of

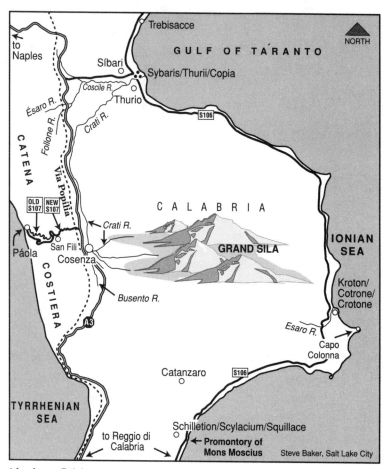

Northern Calabria

lemons found on the trees around the train station. But the modern town now spills down the mountainside to the sea.

Post–World War II buildings are everywhere, bracketing the old city center on three sides; only the steepness of the ever-climbing mountain above protects the top of the old town. I knew I would leave for Cosenza within a few hours, so I checked my luggage at the station and walked a few hundred feet to the beach where the English writer must have disembarked one hundred years earlier.

The beach is stony, but here and there are some patches of sand. There still is no harbor, no dock, no boats tied up. The trainman must have thought my question was indeed odd. A few feet offshore, rusting away in the choppy blue Tyrrhenian, stand round metal casings that must have supported a pier at one time. The beach that Gissing walked up, as the locals, eager for the foreigner's coins, fought over the right to carry his luggage, is now a parking lot.

It was in high surf, just a few yards away from where I stood, that Gissing was lowered from the steamer down to a boat that would carry him to dry land.

"The surf was high; it cost much yelling, leaping, and splashing to gain the dry beach," he wrote. "Meanwhile, not without apprehension, I had eyed the group awaiting our arrival; that they had their eyes on me was obvious, and I knew enough of southern Italians to foresee my reception. I sprang into the midst of a clamorous conflict; half a dozen men were quarrelling over possession of me. No sooner was my luggage on shore than they flung themselves upon it. By what force or authority I know not, one of the fellows triumphed; he turned to me with a satisfied smile, and—presented his wife. '*Mia sposa, signore!*' " Then, Gissing reports, he watched, incredulously, the wife, not the man, grab his steamer trunk, "(a frightful weight), fling it on to her head, and march away at a good speed."

On the day of my visit, this beach was nearly empty except for a few cars with lone occupants sitting and looking seaward, and three bright blue buses used for travel between towns within the region, each waiting to start its schedule. It was a

One hundred years earlier, Gissing marched up this beach at Paola surrounded by townspeople fighting for the privilege of carrying his large steamer trunk. Winning the struggle to carry his possessions was a stout peasant woman, who carried it on the top of her head into the yellow-tinged town high above. *Photo by Paul Paolicelli*

sunny day. The bus drivers stood by their carriage doors, smoking and gazing out to sea.

I was pleased to note that one thing had not changed since Gissing's time: A squat, yellowish, square building, its sign saying DOGANA, or customs house, stood where a predecessor shack might have stood well into the last century when Gissing climbed off the ship and had to have his belongings searched. No such search is required today. It appears the office now is for the *Polizia di finanza*, the fiscal police who ensure that shopkeepers give cash-register receipts to customers, thereby guaranteeing that the transaction is recorded and the State gets its share.

These gray-uniformed officials, though, while they do not

go through a traveler's luggage anymore at every stop, have another role: They seem to prey more on the customers than on the shopkeepers. I had heard for years that I should keep a receipt for even the smallest purchase in Italy until I was several hundred feet beyond the store. These special police are known for stopping purchasers, asking to see the receipt for goods that obviously were just bought, and, if one is not produced, issuing a citation on the spot.

Sometimes shop owners insist on providing the receipt; other times they take the cash, make change without using the cash register, and offer no receipt. After all, if it is rung up on the machine, a record for the tax collector is created. Only once—in a rest-stop coffee bar outside of Naples—have I seen an officer of the *polizia di finanza* watching transactions to ensure they were rung up and receipts dispensed.

The walk up the hill toward the rampart that likely was Gissing's pathway follows modern streets lined with the usual collection of small shops found near the train stations of most Italian cities: a bar serving coffee, a tiny space jammed with hardware, a *barbiere* (barber), a souvenir shop. Pedestrians still use the rampart; cars follow a narrow road that heads straight up along the town's south side.

A pleasing park, with a gratifying view of the Tyrrhenian coast north and south of Paola, sits at the top, and a narrow cobblestone street leads a few hundred feet up to the weathered-stone gate at the entrance to the old town. My predecessor must have walked through this gate. I doubt if any part of the newer town that now lies before it existed one hundred years ago. The gate leads into the old main piazza, Piazza del Popolo, with a grand old fountain at a point where two streets, from the south and north, enter the square. Gissing was deposited at an inn called the *Leone*, the Lion.

He writes: "The room into which they showed me had a delightful prospect. Deep beneath the window lay a wild, leafy garden, and lower on the hillside a lemon orchard shining with yellow fruit. . . . The beauty of this view, and the calm splendor of the early morning, put me into happiest mood. . . . I ate and drank by the window, exulting in what I saw and what I hoped to see."

In an hour's worth of walking around the square, I saw no building identified as the *Leone* nor did I expect to. There was no evidence that an old inn existed in the old town, but I did see gardens where lemon and orange trees flourished in front of buildings facing the sea. This small, old center, with another fountain a few hundred feet down Corso Garibaldi to the north, was charming. The second fountain covered a larger space than the one at Piazza del Popolo. It had several spigots pouring steady streams into the trough-like basin. I could visualize the women Gissing saw drawing "fair water in jugs and jars of antique beauty."

The square was silent. The day was comfortably warm. Birds were in the trees in tiny gardens everywhere. The shocking blue sky had only a few wisps of clouds. The sound of cars— the plague of modern Italy—was distant and easily put out of mind. I could live here, I thought, glancing up at a two-story medieval stone house opposite the tiny square, its back opening from the second level onto a small garden with two orange trees, a lemon tree, and a variety of colorful bushes.

I walked into a small *alimentari*, or grocery store, located just a few feet from this murmuring old fountain and picked out meats and cheeses for a picnic lunch. The two women there

The fountain in Páola's Piazza del Popolo sits in the middle of the old town's one street. This view looks to the south, down via Giuseppe Valitutti. Turn north toward a second, larger fountain with several individual spigots and the street becomes the Corso Garibaldi. The inn Gissing knew as the *Leone* was near this spot. *Photo by John Keahey*

smiled at my attempts to identify the kinds of food I wanted. What do you call "picnic" in Italian? I asked. "Picnic," the woman behind the meat counter said, a broad, warm smile crossing her smooth, unlined face. Months later, I discovered a more appropriate, traditional phrase would have been *una merenda*, an afternoon snack.

I returned to the second fountain—my favorite—and devoured *la mia merenda*: crisp bread holding salami and cheese, a bottle of sparkling water, *con gas* (with bubbles), an orange with its peel streaked dark red—a "blood" orange from the far South, perhaps Sicily. I, like Gissing sitting at his window, was in heaven.

Too soon, I was back at the train station, gathering my luggage and getting ready to board the *locale* for Cosenza. On this trip, the train entered the mountain immediately south of the town, bore through a black tunnel for twenty minutes, and erupted on the east side of the Apennines just north of Cosenza. Disappointing and certainly not a picturesque trip.

Months later, in another journey to this village, I had a car. It made all the difference in following Gissing's trail. The car would keep me out of that dark, uninviting train tunnel. It would allow me to find the old road Gissing followed in his rented carriage. That road, in good repair and still used by locals, appears on some of the more detailed road maps.

Chapter 6

The Missing Madonna, and Concrete Bunkers with a View

The day promised rain. I was looking for the old highway to Cosenza, and the weather was cold. The air had that chilly, wet bite to it that could mean rain might turn to snow. Rain would be no problem, but snow over the tops of the coastal mountains could make the old highway treacherous. With some searching, helpful directions from obliging residents, and a lot of back-tracking, I found the road Gissing used, his small carriage drawn by "three little horses" and his driver accompanied by a "half-naked lad" who, apparently for the fun of it, would leap off the carriage, take "a short-cut up some rugged footway between the loops of the road," and reappear a few minutes later.

Gissing set off from in front of the Leone, where "a considerable number of loafers had assembled to see me off, and of these some half dozen were persevering mendicants [beggars.] It disappointed me that I saw no interesting costume; all wore the common, colorless garb of our destroying age. . . . With whip-cracking and vociferation, amid good-natured farewells from the crowd, we started away. It was just ten o'clock."

The road his carriage driver followed up and over the mountains is the old S107, probably created by the Romans more than one thousand years ago. In recent years, it has been replaced by a new four-lane, freeway-style highway that quickly cuts through the mountains nineteen miles inland to Cosenza, like the train, through its own series of tunnels.

The old road turns sharply off the new highway just a mile or so to the south of Paola. It heads immediately back north and leads a traveler up the incredibly steep mountain, the Catena Costiera, in a series of hairpin curves, climbing higher and higher until I felt almost like I was hanging over the Tyrrhenian coast. The road is paved but extremely narrow, barely wide enough for two cars passing in opposite directions. Some of the hairpin curves are even narrower, so that if two vehicles meet, one would have to stop and wait for the other to pass. And many of the curves are blind where they move around the nose of a promontory.

On this trip over the mountain, I met perhaps four other vehicles coming from the opposite direction. Often, when I stopped to survey the view, I could hear car after car humming along the new highway farther south, their engine noise filtering through the oak, chestnut, beech, and pine trees that, thankfully, shielded them from my view. Except for that distant humming, once over the initial crest of the tall coastal range, I was lost in a deep, silent forest that fascinated me as much as it had the Englishman.

On the steep mountainside, well before I got to the trees, cattle grazed, their bells clanking like deep, hollow-toned wind chimes as they moved through the short grass. The slope was so steep that I imagined those cows must have longer legs on their downhill side.

The new S107 can be seen from the old S107 that carried Gissing in a small
three-horse carriage across the coastal mountains from Paola to Cosenza.
The lichen-covered dome of a German bunker is in the foreground.
Photo by Paul Paolicelli

Midway up, just before the mountain reached a plateau near
where the trees began—Gissing writes that it took three hours
to reach this point; I made it in about twenty minutes—I
stopped at one of the infrequent wide spots along the twisting,
narrow roadway. I beheld the Tyrrhenian Sea. The little town
of Paola, far below and to the north, was shimmering in that
light in such a way that I couldn't separate the modern buildings from the aging, yellow-tinged, centuries-old ones. Gissing
saw such a view, but he did not see in November 1897 what lay
at my feet, just over the edge: a moss-covered, speckled-gray,
cement World War II German machine-gun bunker.

I looked down on the lichen-mottled chamber's rounded
dome just a few feet below me. Then I heard voices behind me.
A group of Italian men, in what appeared to be hunting clothes,
stood on top of a much larger German bunker on the road's

opposite side. They were scanning the mountainside with field glasses, as the Germans must have done fifty-five years earlier. In a few minutes, they climbed into a handful of trucks and cars and sped away down the hill, seemingly oblivious to the blind curves.

The roar of those engines faded. In a few moments the sound of birds came back, and a light wind ruffled the scrubby tops of plants dotting the hillside. Carefully I climbed down into the tiny, doorless bunker. A brown beer bottle lay in the broken rubble on a round floor that perhaps was only a few feet across. The machine-gun portals, of course, looked out toward the sea and the steep hillside below. As far as I know, no battle was fought here: the bulk of the Allied invasion occurred farther north, between Salerno, south of Naples, and Rome. The South suffered a lot of bombing, but not much hand-to-hand combat like farther north.

Through the portals, I could see a portion of the road I had already traveled, twisting serenely below, and the hazy town just beyond.

The curves became fewer as the road undulated, as if over a rolling sea, across the top of the range. Here, I entered the hardwood-and-pine forest. Streams flowed everywhere. Periodically, a religious icon, housed in a small wooden box along the road's side, would come into view. Here and there crosses would appear, shoved into the wet, mossy soil and surrounded by flowers, some dry and withered, some fresh. Each cross had the picture of a Calabrian wearing late-nineteenth or early-twentieth-century garb fastened at the intersection of the wood arms. Gissing wrote of seeing such crosses, but his carriage driver was spooked by them and wanted to hurry on,

A roadside water fountain, deep in the beech and pine forests along the upper reaches of the old S107, depicts San Francesco of Paola, the area's patron saint. Gissing reports seeing a picture of a "blue-hooded" Madonna at this spot. The San Francesco icon appears to have been placed in more recent times. *Photo by John Keahey*

declining to talk about their origins. I assumed these crosses marked the spot of the honored person's death. By accident? By brigands? An Italian friend later told me that usually the deaths recorded by the crosses were indeed caused by accidents along the narrow, twisting roadway. "If the crosses were in memory of someone murdered in those dark mountains," he said, "they would be as thick as a bamboo forest alongside the road!"

At one point, in a curve of the road deep in beeches and oak trees, a small fountain sat at the base of a tiny glen. A pipe, fed by a stream tumbling down through heavy winter foliage in a hillside gully behind, poked out of a large stone slab, and on the slab was a beautiful vertical, tiled image of San Francesco of Paola, the region's patron saint. Gissing wrote that he found

such an image—but a different icon than the one I was seeing—at a spring where the young boy accompanying his driver
drank eagerly from the pipe.

"Now and then he slaked his thirst at a stone fountain by the
wayside, not without reverencing the blue-hooded Madonna
painted over it." The likeness I saw of San Francesco, set in
brightly painted tiles, appeared to be of more recent origin. I
hoped this was the same spot Gissing described and that only
the icons had changed. Once again I could share a moment during this "long, wild ascent" with the English writer who died
forty-two years before I was born, his thin, wiry Calabrian carriage driver, and a small boy whose "breath and muscle" Gissing
envied while "[p]erspiring, even as I sat, in the blaze of the sun."

I drank from the pipe. The water was so cold I could almost
feel my teeth crack. What a treat this would be on a hot day following a climb up a dusty road in a three-horse carriage. I
thought about the young boy, who now would be well over a
century old, and I thought about a time when I was sixteen,
attending a camp in the Idaho mountains. A group of friends and
I ran straight up a mountainside for, what seems in the foggy
memory of time, at least half an hour, without stopping. We
reached a tall cross, as tall as a person, planted like the Italian
boy's Madonna deep into the soil, touched it, and immediately
turned around and headed downhill, leaping as we ran, springing
from rock to rock, fallen tree trunk to tree trunk, like the gazelles
on cable television's nature shows. I remember that time four
decades ago with amazement, realizing that we were barely
breathing hard when we reached our camp at the bottom.

Here, I felt perspiration rolling down my neck, despite the
cold, cloudy day that still threatened rain, as I walked back up
a slight incline a few hundred feet to my car, my legs aching

from the effort. I climbed in and headed on the freshly paved road toward the summit and the Ionian Sea beyond.

Periodically, perhaps every ten miles or so, a structure of jumbled stones would appear, looking like the ruins of old Roman way stations that one occasionally finds while following modern highways that follow the same paths as the ancient roads. Did the Romans build this road to connect the sea with the Crati valley inland? It certainly is not straight, as Roman roads tend to be—even those that go straight up the sides of hills— the easier to move foot soldiers marching in formation. To make a nearly straight road in these mountains would have been impossible. Occasionally, there also would be abandoned structures of more recent origin. The faded word RISTORANTE was over the door, hanging from one hinge, of one such empty structure, its glass windows missing and heaps of rubble piled inside. These, I figured, were roadside businesses forced to close when old S107, Gissing's and my route, was replaced by the modern, faster, more efficient—but certainly less serene— new S107.

On the downhill side, heading toward the small village of San Fili, I passed two large trucks parked facing me just off the road. They were loaded with freshly cut beech logs, removed from the gently sloping hillside above. Every few feet or so, a tree had been left standing, to replenish, I assume, another harvest a few decades from now. Farther down the road, an elderly man was piling branches and other wooden refuse left by the loggers into a smaller truck. He looked up, his arms wrapped around a bundle of branches, and acknowledged my wave with a curt nod.

Eventually, I came down into San Fili, where Gissing's driver had dropped off a small wagon to be repaired. This is where the old road rejoins the new highway and heads nearly straight as an arrow past the village.

Near this point, the main A3 Autostrada into Cosenza follows the path of an old Roman road—a road over which passed the Visigoth Alaric, fresh from his most recent early-fifth-century-C.E. sack of weak and declining Rome, which was then the befuddled, decadent capital of the Western Empire. The Eastern Empire had earlier been moved to Constantinople, dividing the power of the once mighty Romans.

Alaric was leading his army, heavily laden with the Eternal City's remaining booty, toward Sicily, his proposed base for an attack into North Africa. He never made it; his story ends in Cosenza just ahead.

Gissing's feelings about following such a historic route were similar to the ones I had during this fine, clear moment—the clouds threatening rain had disappeared—on the slopes overlooking the Crati River valley. There is something ethereal about standing on a spot over which ancients passed millennia ago. I also had learned from the Englishman that this same route—the Via Popilia, now the A3—was followed by Carthaginian general Hannibal six hundred years before Alaric.

Ahead was Cosenza, known in Roman times as Consentia. Its founding goes back to the prehistoric hill tribe, the Bruttians, who were there thousands of years before the Greeks set foot on the southern part of the Italian peninsula. And through this Calabrian city flow two rivers: the Busento, which merges into the mighty Crati at the old town's base. From there, the Crati, famous since antiquity, flows past other, still buried, ancient cities on its way to the Ionian Sea.

Chapter 7

Cosenza

At precisely four in the afternoon, Cosenza loomed outside my window, the old town scurrying up the foothills of the Grand Sila, lit by the west-setting sun that was preparing to disappear behind the mountain range I had just crossed. This was the same time of day Gissing arrived, barely more than one hundred years earlier. He had left Paola, leaving by carriage from in front of the *Leone* at ten o'clock that morning. His journey along the old, winding Paola–Cosenza road took six hours; it now takes travelers about thirty minutes by train through a tunnel in the Catena Costiera mountains. I drove it in just over an hour by car, including several stops.

The Greeks had problems with the native peoples—the Bruttians—who made this their capital deep in the heart of Calabria. This region, in fact, was known as Bruttia in those days. It did not become known as Calabria until the Byzantine era, long after the Greeks were vanquished by the Romans and Rome itself was in decline.

According to Margaret Guido, who wrote *Southern Italy: An*

Archaeological Guide, the tribes the Greeks encountered when they began establishing colonies along the south and west coasts of southern Italy had, over time, become less distinct from one another. Collectively, those who had been the Ausonians or the proto-Villanovans became known as the Bruttians. The Bruttians, from their capital at Cosenza, constantly harassed the Greeks. Later, when the Romans arrived, the conquerors wisely tried to assimilate these wild mountain people, but their plans, Guido tells us, were delayed while the Romans fought Hannibal, and assimilation "was only achieved after his withdrawal."

Cosenza's *città nuova* (new town) developed over the decades after Gissing's visit in the fall of 1897, and much of it following World War II, when it was bombed heavily. Where modern buildings and streets now stand, he likely saw wide-open farmland sweeping northward through the center of the Italian peninsula's southern half.

Of course Gissing's inn in this high-mountain community, the *Due Leonetti*, or Two Little Lions, does not exist today in name, although the building likely survives. Gissing was not one for listing addresses—not unusual for someone writing a memoir rather than a guidebook.

After I unloaded baggage at my hotel room in the modern part of town, I crossed over the Busento River and into the old city, where I walked up streets still as narrow as one hundred years earlier. I hoped to see old, fading paint declaring the name, or at least representations in stone, of two tiny lions. No such luck.

But no doubt one of the buildings I passed had once contained the *Leonetti*. Gissing wrote that when his driver deposited him at the front door, "Over sloppy stones, in an atmosphere heavy with indescribable stenches, I felt rather than saw my way to the

Gissing did not like the looks of the railroad bridge over the confluence of the Busento and Crati Rivers at the bottom of Cosenza's old town. He alluded to its ugliness in front of the millennia-old Calabrian village. Now a modern building blocks the panorama of the old city near the spot originally settled by native Bruttian peoples. The Crati River flows in from the left; the Busento, where the bones of Alaric the Visigoth are believed buried, flows in from the right to fortify the Crati for its journey northeastward to the Ionian Sea.

Photo by John Keahey

foot of a stone staircase. . . . The room itself was utterly depressing—so bare, so grimy, so dark. Quickly I examined the bed, and was rewarded. It is the good point of Italian inns; be the house and the room howsoever sordid, the bed is almost invariably clean and comfortable."

Instead of the tiny hotel, I found a delightful old town with tall, multistoried structures that created dark caverns where the sun, briefly at high noon, struggles to enter. There were no stenches. My experience was a glorious blend of odors coming from bubbling pots of sauces, pasta, meat, and fish being tended deep inside these dark, frightfully old buildings.

Eventually, I walked out into a large, sunny square—the

Piazza XV Marzo, a relief from the dark, narrow slots between the buildings of the old town below. It had to be the same wide-open square Gissing described, so dramatic is the transition from the deep caverns of the town to this promontory.

Workers were renovating a public building on the north edge, and a freshly painted theater, looking to be at least a century old, occupied a position opposite. Beyond lay a garden, with tall trees, still holding in winter their leafy canopy. The garden was terraced on a hillside, and small fountains with nymphs carved from white stone were positioned throughout. I found this park, so clearly described in Gissing's book, during my second visit, just a few months after the first. In that initial trip, I had mistakenly looked for this garden on the opposite side of town.

During that first foray into Calabria's interior, I had asked a fellow passenger on a Cosenza city bus which river we were crossing. "*Il Busento,*" he replied, not looking up from his paper. So for the rest of that journey, I believed that the Busento came out of the mountains east of the town and that the Crati flowed along the west side before the convergence of the two rivers at the city's north edge. The park simply was not where it should be if the man on the bus was correct. And why shouldn't he be? He lives here, I thought to myself.

It took a second visit to solve the mystery. When I stumbled into the garden near the top of the sunny piazza, I was sure I had caught Gissing in a factual error. He said the garden looked over the Crati. The bus passenger months earlier told me this was the Busento.

A construction worker solved the puzzle. I asked if the Busento was indeed below the garden. "No, no," he said. "It is the Crati." Later, I asked schoolchildren playing along the river's bank: "What river is this?" "The Crati!" they shouted, one after the other. Then, I did the obvious: I consulted a map, something I had failed to do months earlier.

Indeed, the Crati flows from the east, the Busento from the southwest. I had been gazing upstream at the wrong river.

I walked back into the park. Regrettably, the view in the late 1990s was significantly different from that in the late 1890s. It is impossible, from the park's heavily wooded slopes, to catch a glimpse today of "the yellow gorge of the Crati." Tall buildings are rooted along the park's base, between it and the river. And buildings are piled up on the opposite bank, masking the fact that the channel exists. The eye only sees one unbroken stretch of town. Over the flow of modern traffic below, I could not hear the gurgling river from the city garden, as Gissing did. Nor could I grab a view of its junction with the Busento, just barely a half mile away.

The newly reinforced Crati follows the valley northward toward the final battlefield of the Roman gladiator and rebel-slave leader Spartacus, and the narrow tract of land between the Ionian and Tyrrhenian Seas.

Progress has left its mark on this town as elsewhere in the South. Cosenza periodically has been devastated by earthquakes, including one in 1905, eight years after Gissing's visit. That means new buildings forced on top of old, not to mention what must have replaced structures leveled during World War II bombing runs.

Disappointed at not being able to see the Crati from the same viewpoint Gissing used one hundred years earlier, I walked down and out of the garden and wove my way through twentieth-century streets toward the Crati and Busento junction. Gissing saw it "in the light of sunrise, the Busento flowing amid low, brown, olive-covered hills"—hills that now are covered by tall buildings.

Somewhere in the bed of the nearby Busento, probably within shouting distance, lay the grave of Alaric the Visigoth, who, after despoiling Rome, led his army along the Roman road, the Via Popilia, whose path I saw from San Fili. He died, likely of malaria. His story and his place in Cosenza's history are unique.

Gissing was well aware of Alaric and his impact on the Western world. The English writer, steeped in the classics since childhood and in Gibbon's great eighteenth-century work *The Decline and Fall of the Roman Empire*, knew that the chief of the Visigoths was born in what is now Romania in C.E. 370 and led the final sack of Rome in August 410. That event, writes Gibbon, signified the fall of the Western Empire.

Alaric had been an officer in the Roman army, and later defected to become chief of his native tribe. Unhappy that his people had not received tribute promised by the Romans, he proceeded to ravage the eastern lands held by his former master.

Nine years before his death in 410 C.E. at about age forty, Alaric invaded Italy for the first of two defeats at the hands of the Romans. The mistake Rome made in the third confrontation was to adopt an anti-barbarian political position—no negotiations, no surrender—and to launch a wholesale slaughter of wives and children of tribesmen serving in the Roman army. These soldiers defected to Alaric, and his army grew. Ancient writers say Alaric wanted peace, but the Roman emperor Flavius Honorius would have nothing to do with the Visigoth.

Alaric besieged Rome the first time in C.E. 408, and the Senate sued for peace. When Honorius still balked at recognizing the Visigoth and paying tribute, Alaric surrounded the city again in 409. He cut off all supplies to the city, and widespread starvation hit the inhabitants.

Historian J. B. Bury reports that Rome was "reduced to such extremities of starvation, that someone cried in the circus, *Pretium impone carni humanae*, [Latin for] 'set a price on human flesh.'" Negotiations resumed, breaking down a third time. So another siege was launched, and this time, on August 24, C.E. 410, Alaric entered a city that had not been captured by a foreign enemy, Gibbon says, for six hundred and nineteen years. He was not benevolent. Bury reports: "He allowed his followers to slay, burn, and pillage at will. The sack lasted for two or three days."

It had been brutal. Rome's walls in the early fifth century C.E. covered twenty-one miles. Gibbon dutifully reports there were 48,382 houses in the city. Alaric's troops had surrounded Rome, blocked all gates, and controlled the flow of commerce in the Tiber, effectively preventing provisions from reaching the citizens. Gibbon says: "The first emotions of the nobles and of the people were those of surprise and indignation that a vile barbarian should dare to insult the capital of the world; but their arrogance was soon humbled."

A paragraph later, Gibbon reports: "The unfortunate city gradually experienced the distress of scarcity and at length the horrid calamities of famine." As the third siege pressed on, "Many thousands of the inhabitants of Rome expired in their houses or in the streets for want of sustenance; and as the public [cemeteries] without the walls were in the power of the enemy, the stench which rose from so many putrid and unburied carcasses infected the air."

Finally, the beleaguered Senate opened negotiations. Alaric's ransom to free the city eventually reached the payment of five thousand pounds of gold, thirty thousand pounds of silver, four thousand robes of silk, three thousand pieces of fine scarlet cloth, and three thousand pounds of pepper. The Visigoths took these riches, went a short distance north to what is now Tuscany, and later turned south, hoping to reach Sicily and launch an attack on North Africa.

After overpowering towns en route to Sicily but abandoning an unsuccessful siege at Naples, Alaric and his army reached Rhegium (modern Reggio di Calabria), in Italy's toe. There, ships lay at anchor to carry the Visigoths to Sicily. But a storm hit, wrecking the ships in the strait. Alaric was forced to backtrack. Bury speculates that Alaric may have wanted to return to Naples, capture the city, and raise a fleet there. But when Alaric once again passed Cosenza on his return north, he died "before the end of the year (C.E. 410)."

The Visigoth chieftain likely was bitten by the wrong mosquito and contracted malaria as so many tens of thousands of southern Italians have done over the centuries.

The rest of the story is the intriguing part. It fascinated Gissing, who began his trip into Magna Graecia to see Greek cities but adjusted this itinerary to explore Alaric's fabled place of burial. The story also fascinates historians and archaeologists, who would like to explore the Visigoth's river-drenched tomb, if ever it could be found. While ancient writings describe *what* happened, no one knows precisely *where* it happened. If the myths are true, a gigantic booty of Rome's treasure awaits its discoverer, along with Alaric's bones.

The legends report that when Alaric died, his army temporarily diverted the Busento River near where it joins the Crati at the base of Cosenza's old town. They then buried him, along with gold and other Roman riches, in the muddy riverbed, and then restored the waters to their regular channel, forever obliterating the grave. Some sources say the soldiers then slaughtered the townspeople who helped, so no one could reveal the grave's location. Gissing and others dispute this, saying the tomb was likely dug out of sight of the town, farther upstream, and therefore in secret.

I stood at the confluence of the two rivers. On the north bank of what I now knew to be the Crati, along a commercial sidewalk just a few hundred feet from its confluence with the Busento, stands a bust of a sixteenth-century Albanian prince. Its origin appears recent, and it has been defaced with dark red spray paint. People I spoke with indicate that no one really knows for sure the precise location of the confluence in Alaric's time. It could be farther upstream or, perhaps, even farther downstream. And it would be difficult to determine the location of either river's channel nearly one thousand six hundred years ago.

Today, both riverbeds are contained, against roaring spring floods, within concrete walls. The rivers can no longer meander at will as they did through geologic time. In ancient times, those river channels could have been anywhere through land now covered by twentieth-century buildings.

I had to gaze up the Busento—like Gissing, and the historians and archaeologists before and after him—toward its hidden source in the Grand Sila and speculate. Gissing saw women washing their clothes in the riverbeds. I saw plastic milk bottles bobbing in the shallow current, along with beat-up aluminum chairs, the rusted steel springs of a bed, and disintegrating pieces of cardboard boxes.

I walked to the first bridge that crosses the newly combined river Crati just below the present-day confluence and, with the centuries-old town at my back, looked northward along the Crati valley. My eyes could follow the river through the haze of modern Calabria for only a few miles as the river flowed toward the Ionian Sea. There, at its mouth, the ancient Greek city of Sybaris would be founded in 720 B.C.E., eleven hundred and thirty years before the fall of Rome and Alaric's fatal illness.

Chapter 8

Where Spartacus Fell

Shaking off the early morning chill from my walk to Cosenza's *stazione*, I descended by train from the town that native Bruttian tribesmen built millennia ago, snug against the slopes of the still snow-covered Grand Sila. Once under way, the train dropped down through a wide, rolling valley sculpted by the Crati and other rivers, all springing from Apennine slopes and draining this fertile land on their way to the Ionian Sea.

The train and the historic Crati, both heading north, intersect ancient pathways across this narrow part of Italy. One such pathway runs near where the river turns northeastward toward Sibari, and near the point where the Esaro and Follone Rivers join to flow into the Coscile, which in turn flows into the Crati.

That ancient route, now followed in part by the A3 Autostrada, was in Roman times a section of the Via Popilia. The ancients from Copia to the east who turned south on that old road would end up in Rhegium, modern Reggio di Calabria, in Italy's toe. If they turned north, they could connect with the Via Appia and Via Latina at Cápua, north of Naples, both leading to Rome. Heading east from its intersection with the Popilia, the Appia initially ended at Tarentum—formerly the Greek city Taras established in the eighth century B.C.E. and now called Taranto—some one hundred sixty miles from Rome. The Appia later was extended past Tarentum to Brundisium, now Brindisi, on the Adriatic coast.

Probably the first people to use these ancient tracts three thousand or more years ago—long before the Romans paved and named them—were local tribes. They were on the land for centuries before Greek colonists, in the eighth century B.C.E., set foot on the coast of southern Italy, naming their western colonies Magna Graecia.

Seeing this much-used land, now covered by pastures of sheep and dotted with orange and lemon groves, provides perspective. As an American, and particularly as a western American, my concept of "old" had been the tiny log cabin—now held together by modern glue and on display for tourists—built by the first white settlers in my valley one hundred and fifty years ago. If I really want to reach into the pre-pioneer past of my region, I can look at the "old" Fremont and Anasazi ruins vacated in the southwestern United States as long ago as C.E. 1100, a time when pre-Renaissance painters were working in Italy. I live in a house, referred to as "old" by Americans, that was built in 1915, a blink of only eighty-five years!

I remembered my first Italian-language teacher in Siena, listening to me, her face holding a sardonic smile, as I proudly talked about how old my home was and how I was renovating it. She said, matter-of-factly, that her home just outside of Siena's walls dated back to the twelfth century C.E. It had been renovated dozens of times in the intervening seven hundred years. And there was another teacher who, leading me up the steps to her Sienese office eighteen months later, casually mentioned that the three-foot-high vase in the entryway, with flowers tumbling from the top, was, probably, several hundred years old. "It has always been here," she said, shrugging off questions about its origins.

Now, far away from Siena, I watch this historical stretch across the Apennine range between the Ionian and Tyrrhenian Seas reveal itself through the window of my train compartment. In addition to the Bronze Age and Iron Age peoples who walked here, this area also was used heavily by early Greek colonists-turned-traders.

About 720 B.C.E., one group of Greeks built the city of Sybaris between the rivers Coscile (called the Sybaris River in ancient times) and Crati, at a point near where both flowed just hundreds of yards apart into the Ionian Sea. This city became famous in ancient times for its wealth and the hedonistic, gluttonous lifestyle of its citizens. It is this city's ancient name that gives us the English word *sybarite*, used to describe someone who is a voluptuary or a sensualist.

Today's Coscile has lost its Ionian mouth and now flows into the Crati some thirteen miles west of the ancient city of Sybaris's recently discovered location. The archaeological dig is just southeast of modern Síbari along the main road, S106, that connects Taranto to the north and Reggio to the south.

Ancient writers say the tract westward from Sybaris to the Tyrrhenian Sea could be traveled with pack animals in just three days, allowing Sybarite traders to connect with Etruscan traders, who sailed south along the west coast from the region of modern Tuscany north of Rome. This trade took place in a series of colonies—Poseidonia, Skidros, and Laos. Poseidonia, now well preserved and known by its later Roman name Paestum, is part of a complex of ruins sixty miles south of Naples.

The pathway between Sybaris and its west-coast subcolonies crosses ground near where Spartacus fought and died in 71 B.C.E. Hollywood, in the Stanley Kubrick film *Spartacus*, had the gladiator, believed to be a former Roman army officer, dying instead on a cross near Rome. But his death, historians tell us, was likely on the battlefield near the Crati and in the midst of a plain traversed for thousands of years before his birth.

Spartacus's followers were taken to Capua—the site of the gladiatorial school north of Naples where he had been trained—and were crucified by the thousands, one after another, along the Via Appia between there and the southern gates of then Republican Rome.

Today at the former Greek subcolony of Poseidonia, now called Paestum, it is hard to imagine that these magnificent ruins were virtually unknown until the eighteenth century C.E. Margaret Guido, writing in *Southern Italy: An Archaeological Guide*, tells us that these "splendid Greek temples" for hundreds of years had been "hidden among trees and malarial swamps, which in the course of centuries developed around them. They may even have been partly standing in water."

Today, we see the remains of a nearly complete Greek town, generally "unencumbered by modern building, though modified and added to in Roman times."

Guido offers a clue as to why the Greeks flourished for so many centuries in a land that eventually became swampy and beset with malaria, driving its occupants elsewhere.

Since early ancient times, she notes, the trees that blanketed the region had been cut down. Rivers, such as the Sele, that flow near Poseidonia/Paestum became silted up with a sediment of rocks and mud brought down from the denuded hills, "and gradually the site became more and more infested with malaria." This affliction has led to the deaths in southern Italy of tens of thousands over the centuries. Along with a continual flow of invaders, malaria forced people out of the coastal plains and into the high Calabrian and Basilicatan mountains, creating the hilltop fortresses tourists find so appealing.

Guido continues, "In medieval times a few Christians were still worshipping in the Temple of Ceres. . . . But soon after, the forests and swamps encroached and finally hid it for centuries."

Uncovered at Paestum, which retains the name the Romans gave it when they refounded Greek Poseidonia in 273 B.C.E., are three temples. Two were shrouded in scaffolding in the late 1990s as preservationists worked to clean and preserve the structures. The oldest of these, the temple closest to the sea, dates back to the sixth century B.C.E., and was probably dedicated to the goddess Hera.

It seems that nearly every ancient Greek city had a temple dedicated to Hera, including the one at Paestum, and others at Metaponto and near Crotone, both towns on Gissing's, and my, agenda. Little wonder. As the wife of Zeus, she was a major figure in the Greek pantheon of gods that dates back to the Mycenaeans, who dominated what became mainland Greece for several hundred years.

Authors of *The Oxford Classical Dictionary* note that "the most ancient and important temples were those of Hera. Her cults also spread at an early date to the colonies of the west, where later she became identified with the Roman Juno. Her sanctuaries at the Lacinian promontory [near Kroton/Cotrone/Crotone] and at [Paestum] were much frequented."

Alongside Hera's temple at Paestum is one dedicated to Neptune, likely built in 475 B.C.E. There also are foundations of buildings, old city streets, the outline of a forum dating to the later Roman times, an amphitheater cut through the middle by the modern road, and well-preserved walls that go back to the late Greek period or to the time when native tribes, in the late fifth century B.C.E., conquered the city and drove out the Greeks.

A short distance to the west is the Tyrrhenian Sea. There, when the city was known as Greek Poseidonia, and at the other ports, Etruscans arrived from the north to exchange their goods for Greek wares.

The Sybarites developed the overland route connecting Sybaris to Poseidonia, Skidros, and Laos. Historians today refer to this tract as the Sala Consilinum. It was developed, in part, so the traders could avoid a long, perilous, pirate-laden Mediterranean journey to the Tyrrhenian Sea that would have led them around Sicily, or through what is known as the Strait of Messina, where Italy's toe nearly touches Sicily.

Two millennia later, the Panama Canal would serve a similar purpose in the Americas.

This was a sophisticated, symbiotic system of trade that began hundreds of years before the Romans shook off their kings, consolidated their hold on the hills that made up that ancient village, and became a republic. Centuries still remained before the armies of that republic would unify all of Italy, or the Roman Empire, much later, could comprehend domination of the Mediterranean world.

In fact, the late-eighth-century-B.C.E. establishment of the colony at Sybaris corresponds roughly with the time given for Romulus's mythical founding of Rome. That date reflects how much more advanced the Greeks were as a western civilization than their eventual conquerors, the Romans. We have ancient writings that describe Sybaris; only myths hint at the establishment of Rome.

For my trip one hundred years after Gissing's, the rain held off, and as the train and I trundled closer to sea level from the heart of interior Calabria, yellow spring flowers—millions of them that later, upon closer inspection, appeared to be broom plants, or *genista*—started appearing across the fertile river plain. The prospects for a sunny day increased as we went first northward, crossing over the ancient Ionian–Tyrrhenian tract, and then northeastward.

The train approached Sibari and the ruins of the ancient Greek colony Sybaris and its successor Greek colony of Thurii. Recent excavations at the site have identified a third and more recent city, the Roman town of Copia, built over the ruins of its predecessor Greek cities.

Thurii, settled more than six decades after Sybaris was destroyed by rivals from the nearby Greek colony of Kroton, was the last stronghold of the doomed Spartacus. Thurii also was where, nearly three hundred and fifty years before the rebel-slave leader's time, the ancient world's first western historian, Herodotus, died—about 425 B.C.E.

Some chafe at calling Herodotus a historian. To James Romm, who wrote an impressive study of the ancient writer, his life, times, and methods, Herodotus was moralist, storyteller, dramatist, student of human nature, perhaps even journalist. The book, titled simply *Herodotus*, is not a biography because nearly nothing is known about the man's life, other than a few personal insights contained within Herodotus's seminal work, the *Histories*.

We do know he lived through much of the fifth century B.C.E., about 485 to 425, and about three hundred years after Homer, who wrote the *Iliad* and the *Odyssey*. As Romm points out, that span of three centuries between the two writers is about the same span that separates writers today from John Milton, who wrote *Paradise Lost*. The ancients would have seen the same kind of difference between Homer's and Herodotus's styles that we see today between Milton's complex form and Ernest Hemingway's terse, direct prose.

Homer wrote in verse, the universal written art form of the time; Herodotus wrote prose, which Romm says was a little-used, or second-class, art form the Greeks referred to as " 'naked language' (lacking the decorous 'clothing' supplied by meter) . . . [or as] 'language that walks on foot' (as opposed to riding in poetry's winged chariot)."

Up to the time of Herodotus, poets recounted myths crediting the gods with controlling all events. With Herodotus, "no longer can the muse be invoked as guarantor of authenticity," Romm tells us. Instead, Herodotus calls upon "human powers of investigation and reason" to replace the role of the gods.

All we really know about Herodotus's place of birth is the clue he gives us in his original opening line of the *Histories*: "This is the setting-forth of the research of Herodotus of Halicarnassus, so that the things arising from humankind may not be dulled by time, and that great and wondrous deeds displayed by both Greeks and barbarians may not lose their renown, as regards other things and through what cause they made war upon one another." This quote is from the translation Romm used. Other translators convey those same opening remarks, but often with the sentence's clauses in different order.

Halicarnassus was a Greek city on the southwest coast of

Turkey, within the Greek colony of Ionia, colonized around the same time as southern Italy to the west. In a later edition of the *Histories,* produced in the fourth century B.C.E. and quoted by Aristotle, according to Romm, Herodotus identifies himself in that famous first sentence as being "of Thurii," the Greek city rebuilt from the stones of Sybaris and later supplanted by Roman Copia. If true, these two scant geographical references mean he spent his youth "on the eastern perimeter of the Greek world and his maturity in the far west."

Herodotus appears to be an extensive traveler, writing about events and describing sites that existed prior to his birth. But he rarely describes the journeys themselves. "It would be as though Marco Polo, in medieval Italy, had given his account of China without saying anything about the journey there or back!" Romm says. Of course, the critic writes, some scholars explain this dearth of travel description by accusing Herodotus, as Marco Polo has been accused, of "inventing most of all of his travels."

Romm tells us that Herodotus migrated to Thurii when he was well into his forties, and that he likely had written most of his *Histories* by that time, although it is believed that he was still adding to it at the time of his death. But there still remains some question as to whether he died there:

"Thurii was said by some to contain Herodotus's grave, indicating perhaps that he remained there until his death, sometime after 430 (B.C.E.); but another city, Pella in Macedonia, also claimed his remains, so he may have left the golden west to return to the Greek mainland."

In Gissing's time, remains of Sybaris/Thurii/Copia had not yet been found. Historians generally agree that in 510 B.C.E. the enemies from Kroton (called Cotrone at the time of Gissing's visit in the late 1800s, and changed to Crotone in 1928) razed the city by breaching retaining walls built by the original settlers to hold back the Crati just west of where the waterway emptied into the sea. The deluge completely flooded Sybaris and obliterated one of Magna Graecia's most magnificent cities after a mere 210 years of life.

Then, sixty-six years later, in 444 B.C.E., on the orders of Pericles of Athens, the southern Italian Greeks re-established the city, naming it Thurii. A few years after Rome's war with Hannibal two centuries later, Rome began building in 193 B.C.E. what it named Copia, using as building blocks the remains of the two earlier Greek towns. After Copia was abandoned, its remains were buried to a depth of at least twenty feet by more than two thousand years' accumulation of alluvial mud and silt.

For more than one hundred years, modern archaeologists had speculated about where Sybaris/Thurii/Copia lay, but major excavations did not begin until the mid-twentieth century, some six decades after Gissing's visit.

Chapter 9

Searching for Sybaris

The tiny modern-day hamlet Sibari is where, in late 1897 during a brief train layover en route to Taranto, Gissing enjoyed lunch after his early morning departure from Cosenza. He likely munched bread and drank wine just a few miles from where the archaeological dig at Sybaris/Thurii/Copia would begin in earnest more than a half century later. When leaving Taranto and heading days later toward Cotrone (today Crotone), his train passed within shouting distance of where the three ancient cities, the last two built from their predecessors' stones, are today being unearthed.

I wanted to visit these digs and see what Gissing had been unable, but yearned, to see. Driving north toward Sibari across miles and miles of flat, coastal plain, I realized that S106, a two-lane modern highway, was cutting through the middle of an archaeological dig. Excavations revealing stone foundations spread out on both sides of the highway. Ahead, to the north, a road turned west into the archaeological park. I went in, parked, and started walking toward the dig, my camera strapped around my neck.

A voice stopped me. *"É chiuso!"* It's closed. "There is too much water. It is dangerous," said a man who was leaning out of the doorway of a long, one-story wooden building. I walked toward him, saying I needed photographs for a book. "If the pictures are to be published you need special permission. Go to the museum," he said, pointing north up the road.

For a brief moment, I contemplated just going back to S106, taking pictures as any tourist would from a turnoff. But something told me to play it straight. *"Mille grazie,"* Thank you, I said to the earnest young man.

The museum, just off S106, east toward the Ionian Sea, is a modern structure that is one of the finest museums of its type. Its lighting is a major departure from that found in musty, centuries-old buildings that traditionally house ancient artifacts, and its display spaces are flexible. Many different types of exhibits can be set up, changed, and moved easily.

I walked inside and paid my four-thousand-lira (about two dollars and forty cents) entrance fee and asked who I needed to talk to for permission to take photographs of the archaeological site. The attendant shook his head. Written permission must be gotten from some official in some distant city. I felt defeat coming on, but decided to tour the museum while pondering whether to take the pictures from the road as I originally planned.

Then, just as I was walking up a ramp to the first exhibit room, a delightful woman, short in stature with a pixie-like haircut and sparkling eyes, approached. "May I help you?" she asked in perfect English, spoken with a distinct British accent.

I explained my mission. She smiled and said, "I will give you

The Crati River once inundated this stone road in the heart of the Park of the Horse in the ancient Greek city of Sybaris, established in 720 B.C.E. and flooded by warriors from nearby Kroton in 510 B.C.E. This was the original Greek road, but archaeologists believe a second city, Thurii, was built at this site, followed by the later Roman city of Copia. The pipes on the left are attached to pumps that must operate around the clock to keep ground water from once again flooding the site. *Photo by Paul Paolicelli*

a tour even though the park is closed today. You can take all the photos you want!"

Isora Migliari described herself as a "technical assistant" at the excavations, where she has worked for the past eighteen years. Everything we were looking at, she said—stone foundations, paving stones for streets, a few pieces of columns scattered here and there, pieces of mosaic floors, an amphitheater—dated to the Roman-era town of Copia. If the predecessor Greek cities of Thurii or Sybaris, far underneath Copia, were ever to be uncovered, the Roman ruins would have to be destroyed. This is not something Italian archaeologists are prepared to do.

The major excavation at Copia is known as Parco del Cavallo,

Park of the Horse. The name was applied because searchers found a set of stone hoofs and a tail, which suggest that a statue of a horse once stood there. It is not known if the statue was of Greek or Roman origin. But horses have a place in the early history of the site. The Greek founders of Sybaris were reputed to be magnificent horse trainers, supposedly training the animals to dance on hind feet to tunes played on reed pipes. This, if ancient writers are to be believed, helped lead to the undoing of Sybaris. The Krotonians knew about the dancing horses, so the legend goes, and when they fought the Sybarites, Kroton warriors blew songs through pipes, and the horses of the city's defenders began to rear up and dance, making it impossible for the mounted Sybarites to fight and save the city.

Farther to the east and closer to the Ionian shoreline from the *parco*, workers have uncovered the remains of what could have been a structure at the Roman city's wharf area. It is known as Casa Bianca, or White House, only because white stones used in buildings have been uncovered, said Signora Migliari. This site appears to be Roman, with no evidence of either Thurii or Sybaris underneath.

And about one mile north of Parco del Cavallo are the purely Greek ruins identified in modern times as Stombi, or Parco dei Tori, Park of the Bulls. Here, excavators found a small part of the original Sybaris, not impacted by later construction on top. According to a guidebook from the museum at Sibari, there is no evidence of Thurii or Copia at Stombi. But there are "the remains of houses, of the potters' kilns, of the streets and of the everyday objects of the Sybarites."

My friend archaeologist Baldassare Conticello, sitting in his Rome apartment prior to my visit south, shook his head when I asked him about the search for Sybaris. It may be impossible to determine the precise identity of this particular site, he said, because of the overwhelming problem for excavators of water, making the money spent there a subject of controversy.

"Sybaris is in the Ionian Sea," he says, throwing his right hand upward in frustration. Then he explains: It is not the actual sea off the coast of modern-day Sibari he is referring to, but the "sea" under the shoreline, the water that begins filling up the excavations when shovels bite into the earth twenty feet down. He says electric pumps must operate almost continuously to keep the water under control.

"This is the most wasted money ever spent in this country," he says, fuming over the cost of the electrical bill for the continuously running pumps. Indeed, during my visit the park was closed to the general public because of rain and a heavy buildup of groundwater within the excavated area. Several pumps with bright yellow pipes snaking through the area hummed steadily in the background as Signora Migliari showed me the broad stone road, built by the Greeks and used by Romans to move people, wagons, and animals through Copia.

"Don't step there," she advised me as we neared low stone walls surrounding an area used by the Romans as a public bath. "The ground is saturated and you may fall through." Into what? I thought to myself. The hidden depths of Thurii? Of Sybaris? What an experience that would be!

I had read *Search for Sybaris*, an account of a combined American-Italian dig at the site during the 1960s. This phase in the decades-long search for the city was pursued in part by archaeologists from the Museum of the University of Pennsylvania. Written by Orville H. Bullitt, the now-out-of-print book is an account of the area's history and how excavators, who were

constantly besieged by water filling their excavations, had pinpointed the location of a city. Like the needle in the haystack,
that city—in ancient times likely no more than two square miles
in size—was found within a plain of four hundred square miles.

Bullitt also details how the archaeologists did this. They
used new techniques and equipment, including the magne-
tometer, which records solid material, such as foundation
stones and columns, as deep as twenty feet below the surface.
Bullitt first imagined that these devices would locate the fabled
grave of Alaric the Visigoth, buried in the riverbed of the Crati
before it joined with the Busento at Cosenza.

But it was quickly determined, in the late 1950s and early
1960s, that the search for Alaric, speculated about by Gissing
in the 1890s and by me one hundred years later, was futile,
given how much the town has been built up and how the river's
now rigid course repeatedly shifted in intervening centuries.

So the Pennsylvanians redirected their energies toward the
northeast, to the search for Sybaris. The tie-in with Gissing
was symbolic. He and they first started searching for Alaric,
then moved toward Sybaris. All were connected by the silver
thread of the Crati, which flows over Alaric's bones, and whose
waters were used to bury Sybaris fifty miles from where, centuries before, the Visigoth died.

What those researchers found in the 1960s, however, was
not just Sybaris as they first thought, but the remains of the
newer two cities, built on top. It took other Italian-led excavations to determine that, indeed, the three cities occupied the
same space over the intervening centuries.

In Bullitt's book, published in 1969, Pennsylvanian archaeologist Froelich C. Rainey, then the university's museum director,
wrote in the introduction: "We know now that Sybaris, like

Pompeii, had the misfortune to be located where . . . two great plates of the earth's thin surface collide to cause earthquakes and volcanoes. . . . Today the charred remains of Sybaris lie below a vast blanket of sterile clay sealed in the earth beneath a fertile plain. No wonder it has remained a mystery—no protruding columns, no mounds, no scattered fragments of pottery on the surface to give a clue. Its existence and destruction are hard facts."

It would take archaeologists after the 1960s to tie together the other two cities and explain why Sybaris's columns did not stick up out of the clay: They had become the building blocks of two other cities crumbled by eons of successive earthquakes.

Chapter 10

The Right to Work

The contemporary village of Sibari and its tiny train station had been renamed in the late 1800s from the distracting, unimaginative "Buffaloria." Gissing rejoiced at this, happy that southern Italians, by grasping the Italian versions of ancient names, had finally recognized their Greek roots.

His destination was Taranto, known in antiquity as Taras when founded by the Greeks, and renamed Tarentum by conquering Romans. Taras was one of the earliest extensions of Greece's eighth-century-B.C.E. effort to expand its growing, crowded population to Italy's boot, a process driven by Greece's merchant class, eager to spread commerce around the Mediterranean world. This exodus to Magna Graecia—and also to the east toward Ionia in modern-day southwestern Turkey—was the ancient equivalent of the impact of Europe's "New World" that drew the English, Dutch, French, and Spanish to North America nearly two thousand years later.

The difference here, of course, is that the colonizing Greeks were eventually conquered by the Romans, who grew out of native tribes. These Greeks were either forced out of, or assimilated into, what has become the Italian culture. In North America, it was the other way around: Colonizing Europeans subjugated the original occupants, and European ancestors dominate American culture today.

Southern Italy, according to ancient writers, was viewed as a fertile, undeveloped paradise blanketed by forests and inhabited by groups of Italic tribes—apparently minor obstacles in the path of Greece's early westward expansion.

Coming by train from inland, I first spotted the Ionian Sea just northeast of Sibari and south of Trebisacce. It quickly became the Gulf of Taranto as the train curved northwestward and the bluish gray waters turned deeper blue farther north. The yellow wildflowers were especially heavy here at this lower, warmer elevation. Four days later, when I would head in the opposite direction for a layover at Crotone, they would be double in volume, as spring's warmth spread farther along the coast and into the shoreline's foothills.

The Ionian Sea, while viewed as a separate body of water, is part of the Mediterranean. It is in this sea that the Mediterranean reaches its greatest depth, some sixteen thousand feet at a point off the western coast of Greece, just east of Italy's heel.

Interestingly, the Ionian Sea does not lap up against the portion of southwestern Turkey that had been known as Ionia. *The Oxford Classical Dictionary* speculates that the sea's name originates from early Ionian Greek seafaring to the west. The Ionian's waters touch western Greece, eastern Sicily, and the underside of Italy's boot. A scholar friend points out that Turks refer to Greeks in general as "Ionians."

I sat back as the train moved north along the coast, alone in my compartment like Gissing was in his, reflecting on time and place.

Southern Italy suffers from massive unemployment, as high as thirty-three percent in some provinces, and from domination by political and criminal factions more interested in putting into their pockets the billions of lire the nation has poured southward than in the region's revitalization.

I felt the emotions and saw evidence in the form of angry graffiti that such struggles cause: *Il lavoro è un diritto!* (Work is a right!) was spray-painted in bright red on a brick wall along the tracks near a tiny train station perched on the edge of the Ionian Sea.

I saw the dark, foreboding look in the eyes of a young man who engaged me in an energetic conversation on a bus during a long ride into the countryside. Why are you here? he asked me repeatedly. This is not Rome. This is not Florence, he said, apparently wondering why a tourist would venture so far south from the regular Italian tourist centers. We are poor. Do you come to stare at us?

Then, when my northern Italian–trained ears could no longer follow his rapid-fire southern dialect and I would reply with growing insistence, *"Non capisco, signore. Non capisco"* (I do not understand), he would turn and in loud angry asides say to the bus driver, *"Ricco americano! Ricco americano!"* (Rich American!)

Eventually, I got off that bus with the young man's angry words bouncing off my back. It was upsetting. But over the course of my visit, I began to gauge, at least a little bit, his frustration at living in a land where work and lire are scarce.

I thought of conversations I had in Rome, days before I began my southern journey: one snatched on a bus traveling between the Vatican and the train station. A young Italian air force officer, pointing to an obvious pickpocket on the crowded bus—the notorious *Numero 64* that hauls mostly tourists, prey for pickpockets—winked. With my eye peeled toward the short, stocky thief nervously casing the people around him, I changed the subject. What about the South, I asked. Is it as poor as I hear? I knew the answer, of course. I wanted to see what the young man, obviously gainfully employed in the military, would say.

He identified himself as Valerio and said he was "from the North," adding that he held a typical northerner's view of unemployment and poverty throughout the South.

"In the South it is always the same, no matter what you do," he said in English. "[Southerners] are like that. It will never change." I thought this unusual because I had seen the spray-painted plea for work. Wasn't that a sign that southerners are willing to work?

Later, I recounted this discussion with Professor Baldassare Conticello. He was born in Palermo, so wouldn't he, as a proud Sicilian, dispute the young air force officer's position? The *professore* didn't. He agreed.

"On one side, Italy is the fifth largest economic power. It all comes from the North; on the other [the South], we are a third world nation," Professor Conticello said sadly. "The North is like Switzerland and the South is like Africa! The 'Italian Problem,' I think, cannot be solved."

He continues: "We [in the South] have a sense of dignity and courage, but our limit is to be individualists and reactive to each other." Problem-solving cooperation in the South is hard to come by, he says.

"We are able to discuss with excellent arguments, and for hours, about the beard of Mohammed, but we cannot organize a business!" Northern Italians, he says, "and now even foreigners, profit from our lack of concreteness, and have established a [modern-day recolonization] of southern Italy."

Who is guilty? he asks. Those who do it to the southerners, or the southerners for letting it happen? He does not expect an answer to his question, nor does he offer one.

But the Italian government is trying, once again. In late 1998, the State, driven, says Conticello, by the Communists, created a public agency called *Sviluppo Italia*, Development Italy, that is designed to spark economic growth in the Mezzogiorno. In early 1999, the government named board members known for embracing market values, not politics, according to announcements I read in Italian newspapers.

But this agency "is the daughter of the old *Cassa per il Mezzogiorno*, created in the nineteen fifties by the Social Democrats, and is the granddaughter of an earlier agency, which was created by the Fascists in the nineteen thirties."

The professor remains skeptical of the latest efforts; he has heard all this before. These organizations, with each reincarnation, "are only useful for personal, political, and bureaucratic dishonesty, and for the profusion of organized crime."

Generally, he says, few jobs are created, and despite the billions of lire that have been poured southward, nothing has happened to rectify the imbalance between the Italian North and South.

Visitors to the South often see what I have seen: unfinished freeway ramps hanging out into space, or factories now standing unfinished and empty, that were built for industry—amid much pomp and celebration and fawning newspaper articles—that never came. Much of the money that went south over the last few decades, instead of enhancing the region and its people, ended up in the pockets of crime bosses, bureaucrats, and politicians.

The angry young man who had lashed out at me in frustration on the bus in coastal Calabria cannot be blamed. He was not angry at me personally, the traveler trespassing in his land; his anger was born out of generations of southern hopelessness.

But everywhere in the South, gracious, enthusiastic individuals stand out in greater numbers than the one encounter with that young man. I often think of the cab driver in Táranto—"I am called Giuseppe," he said proudly, as he wrote his name in my notebook—who called me back and pointed to a one-hundred-thousand-lira note (about fifty-seven dollars) I had unknowingly dropped after paying him. I also remember a bus driver at the beginning of my trip. Eager to practice his high-school English learned twenty years earlier, he allowed me to stand in his usually-off-limits-to-passengers driver's area while we sped through the late evening streets that curve around the northern shore of Táranto's Mare Piccolo or Little Sea.

We talked of Greeks, of the wild dogs that, unimpeded by owners or collars, roam Italy's heel and who are fed by locals from garbage pails (*"Sono liberi,"* They are free, he said of those dogs), and of life in America.

"Ah, America," I remember the bus driver saying. "I would like to go there and visit *mio zio*" (my uncle).

"Will you go?" I asked. *"Ci vogliono soldi!"* (You need money!) he replied, rubbing his thumb against his first two fingers—a gesture that means "money" but often is also tinged with the frustration I saw many times as people I spoke with on trains, buses, and in hotel lobbies described life in the South. "Ah," he said wistfully. *"Magari!"* If only!

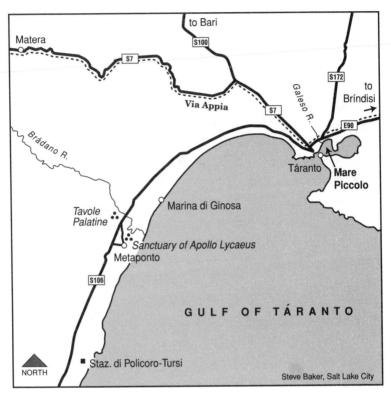

Southern Basilicata/southern Puglia

Chapter 11

Sunlight on old stones

I arrived about midday. Taranto is a strange and wonderful city high on the inside of Italy's heel. From the train station, I took a quick bus ride across a bridge to the island containing the old medieval city that was built on the ruins of Roman Tarentum and Greek Taras. The bus carried me farther east toward a hotel on a side street in the modern downtown, the Albergo Piasi. This new city, *città nuova*, developed across from the southeast end of the island, was connected by a drawbridge.

The old city, the *città vecchia*, is made up of structures dating back to the medieval period. Very little exists from the Roman era, and, near the drawbridge, a single stone column juts into the sky—the only visible evidence that Greeks first settled this spot, and in the light of the setting sun, that column becomes a golden tribute to that era.

In Greek times, the ancient city of Taras, founded in about 706 B.C.E. by colonists from the Greek city of Sparta, ended at a defensive wall near the neck of the peninsula with a ditch located near the point where the canal and drawbridge now sit.

Later, after 275 B.C.E., the Romans took over the city, naming it Tarentum.

Before the ditch was widened into a canal in the Middle Ages, making the city an island, the old city had once been part of the peninsula to the south, between the *Mare Piccolo*, (the Little Sea) and the Gulf of Taranto. It was across this peninsula that Hannibal's soldiers, in 212 B.C.E., used mules to haul ships lashed to wagons from the Little Sea to the Gulf of Taranto and surprise the city's Roman defenders. After Hannibal, the Romans once again re-established their control over the city.

The writer Margaret Guido credits the ancient geographer Strabo with a fine description of the city around the time of the first millennium:

"Evidently the town had a fine gymnasium and a spacious forum still dominated by the huge bronze figure of Zeus. But the acropolis (the upper fortified part of an ancient Greek city), between the forum and the harbor mouth, had already been shorn of most of its former glories. The *via Appia* approached the town by a bridge across the harbor mouth and, having crossed the present *Città Vecchia* and *Città Nuova*, left by a gateway through the walls on the east, just beyond the [cemetery]."

Strabo, a Roman citizen who wrote in Greek and likely was Greek by birth, described the whole of the known world during the reigns of the first two Roman emperors, Augustus and Tiberius. He apparently saw Tarentum long after the Romans had despoiled much of the older Taras to rebuild their own city. Ever the dispassionate observer, I wonder how Strabo must have felt about his older Greek culture's former glories being stripped away at Tarentum.

Taranto became an island some fifteen hundred years later,

in C.E. 480, under Aragonese rulers, far away from their native Spain. The peninsula was breached near the site of the old Greek and Roman defensive walls. It allows a second way into and out of the Little Sea, and it enhanced the city's defenses.

It was precisely that kind of act—the breaching of the peninsula—that would have disturbed the ancient historian Herodotus. I am sure he would have commented on what he considered such an unnatural act had the breach taken place before his time, instead of centuries later, during the Middle Ages.

Herodotus's reaction to a similar act centuries earlier is detailed in his *Histories* and discussed at length in the book *Herodotus* written by James Romm. Herodotus would have considered creating an island from a peninsula to be an act contrary to the structure of the earth, Romm asserts.

What had drawn Herodotus's distaste was the decision by the Persian king Xerxes, who cut a canal across the isthmus of Athos, located in Macedonia, to the northwest of Greece. The king, according to Herodotus, "ordered it to be dug on account of his pridefulness, wishing to display his power and leave a memorial behind; for the Persians could have dragged their ships across the isthmus without taking any trouble at all"— much as Hannibal did at Tarentum. As Romm says, Herodotus "clearly registers disapproval of this alteration of the structure of the earth."

Interestingly, the ancient historian also opposed the structural inverse of such an act. Romm says: It is just as wrong to bridge a strait or a river, since water forms natural boundaries between peoples and territories, "so that to render crossable those that formerly could not be crossed seriously upsets the earth's natural order."

For Herodotus, like many historians since, saw a great struggle over the ages between East and West. When people crossed boundaries between the two, they transgressed "a moral law embedded in the very structure of the earth."

Perhaps Herodotus, who thought nothing of crossing by ship many water boundaries during his travels, had the answer to the question: Why, over so many tens of centuries, has mankind struggled, and continues to struggle, over issues of territory? Perhaps this upsetting of natural balance is why Persia failed to cross from the East into the West effectively and be successful against the Romans. The Romans, dominant in the West, after a period of time also struggled in the East so far away—and across large bodies of water from Rome.

Rome was doomed to fail in Asia. Asia never effectively conquered any significant portion of the West. This certainly remains true today. Herodotus would believe, Romm says, that attempts "to make political geography supersede what is natural" would fail. The Persians perhaps should have stayed in the East, where Herodotus believed they had a more normal and natural place.

"By contrast," Romm says, "the yoking of continents is their [the Persians'] great sin and invites retribution from the gods."

I do not know if the breaching of this peninsula doomed this city to the wrath of the gods, but the island makes Taranto truly unique. I certainly like its atmosphere. On the other side of Taranto's drawbridge, across from the medieval citadel that had been built on top of the Roman citadel where legionnaires held off the invading Hannibal for two years, is the more modern portion of this city. In ancient times, the area contained a necropolis, or burial ground. It eventually became absorbed within the boundaries of the Greek, then Roman, town.

Its tall buildings and wider-than-usual-for-Italy boulevards have developed on a grand scale over the last century since Gissing's visit. In this area one hundred years ago was "a tract of olive orchards and of seedland." This was the land that in ancient times contained Greek tombs.

Here the Englishman had one of his more lyrical encounters: "[T]here, alone amid great bare fields, a countryman was ploughing. The wooden plough, as regards its form, might have been thousands of years old; it was drawn by a little donkey. . . . Never have I seen a man so utterly patient, so primevally deliberate. The donkey's method of ploughing was to pull for one minute, and then rest for two; it excited in the ploughman not the least surprise or resentment. Though he held a long stick in his hand, he never made use of it; at each stoppage, he contemplated the ass, and then gave utterance to a long 'Ah-h-h!' in a note of the most affectionate remonstrance. They were not driver and beast, but comrades in labour. It reposed the mind to look upon them."

The first few streets southeast of the drawbridge look as though they were built in the 1800s. The farther to the southeast I went, across the "olive orchards and seedland" of Gissing's time, the more modern—and more cluttered—the city became.

Somewhere to the north from this spot, along the far shore of the Little Sea—beyond the glistening black sticks that, poking out of the calm water, mark the locations of fishermen's crab pots—was the mouth of the Galeso, a river famous in antiquity and a magnet for Gissing.

He walked to it, carrying visions of its serenity that he had imagined while reading the classical writers. These thoughts must have fed his depression as he yearned to escape into what he perceived to be a simpler, idealized past. I would find that river the next day.

. . .

The Galeso was on the tourist map I picked up the next morning. It was right where Gissing, in his chapter "Dulce Galaesi Flumen" (Sweet River Galeso), said it was. He had walked to the site, but I recruited a cab driver who professed knowledge of the area. The driver—the proud and honest southerner who later pointed to my dropped money—followed the road and rail line that pointed east toward the Adriatic coast. After a few short miles, he stopped on a bridge, raised a finger in the direction of the Little Sea, and said, *"Ecco, il Galeso."*

From this point, the little cattail-choked river lined by giant trees ran perhaps only a short distance to the inner sea. I looked in the opposite direction and saw where the river seemed to come out of nowhere, just a few hundred yards away. Smokestacks of some petroleum center poked up from behind the low hills beyond.

"It rises just over there, from the ground. No other source," Giuseppe said, bending over and moving his open, flat hand up and down a few inches above the pavement.

The river is less than a kilometer (six-tenths of a mile) long, from beginning to end, the cab driver pointed out, seemingly awestruck that such a short body of water could be so famous as to draw an American tourist to its banks.

Except for the giant trees along its length and the sound of humming automobiles from the nearby highway, it was the same river Gissing discovered.

The Englishman wrote that in late 1897, the Galeso flowed through "bare, dusty fields and a few hoary olives." But what I was seeing, one hundred years later, with the trees added and a neatly cultivated farm on one side, was beautiful—more like what the Roman poet Horace might have seen when, in his

The Galeso River, looking
north, springs out of a marsh
shown by the reeds just
beyond the concrete wall.
A petroleum refinery, on the
outskirts of nearby Taranto, is
in the distance. Gissing marveled that this then-
desolate spot and the short,
narrow river were so famous
in classical Greek times.
Photo by Paul Paolicelli

second book of odes, he described the banks of the river
Galaesus as a perfect place to retire, a place where sheep with
fleece so fine browsed along its banks, their valuable coats protected by leather garments.

Giuseppe motioned me back into his cab, breaking my day-
dream. "We go closer," he said. Within a few moments we were
bumping through deserted fields on a weathered dirt road.
With a sudden jerk, he stopped the car. We crawled out of his
tiny cab and stepped onto a concrete bank of the river, directly
below a bridge holding Taranto's main rail line to the Adriatic.
Looking southeast, we saw the river was beautiful, even with
the highway bridge in the distance and the sound of humming
cars floating down to us.

A Sweet and Glorious Land

Turn south, and the mouth of the Galeso, about one-half mile from the river's origin in reeds, empties into Taranto's Little Sea, or *Mare Piccolo*, east of the town. These trees were not here in Gissing's time. He reported seeing only dry dusty fields and a few hoary olives. Along these banks, according to the classical poet Horace, the Greeks grazed their sheep with fleece so fine their coats had to be protected by leather garments. *Photo by Paul Paolicelli*

We stood silent for several moments. Then Giuseppe started talking softly, so softly that I had to ask him to repeat himself. He told me that in 1943, when he was six years old, a British bomb destroyed this rail bridge—at the spot where we were standing—to break this vital supply line to those key Adriatic ports.

"I remember it," he said. "It was a time most unpleasant, but we were glad the British came and the Germans left." After a quiet moment, he chuckled. "Now I drive more German tourists than British, or Americans like you. Only Germans seem to come here now."

His meter was ticking. We left, and I felt the visit to this river had not been long enough. I wanted to walk its short length to where it flowed into the Little Sea.

. . .

For now, I wandered through the medieval city on Taranto's island, making my way back to the hotel across the island's drawbridge. I saw dogs, *i cani liberi*, sniffing through garbage being tossed to them by a man rummaging through a Dumpster. I thought of a line from the classic Sicilian novel *The Leopard*, written in the 1950s by Giuseppe di Lampedusa: "In front of every habitation the rubbish from wretched tables piled up along the leprous walls. Shivering dogs rifled through it, their eagerness always disappointed."

And, as the sky darkened, turning the deep, narrow streets into tunnels lined with faint window-lights, I passed small children shrieking in their games, bouncing balls off the medieval stones on the narrow, dark, and twisting streets. I got lost several times, backtracking repeatedly to regain my bearings.

Only once did I see a dog on a leash. It was a giant German shepherd, pulling its slight owner this way and that. The man was being led by the dog, the animal obviously in charge, despite his tether. He was the only dog I saw over a three-week period that appeared to be tended by any human.

I passed the Greek column, its color now like burnished gold in the glow of a sun just beginning to disappear beyond the sweep of the gulf, and passed the once Roman, now medieval, fort before crossing the drawbridge over the canal. As I walked the block or so into the crest of the newer city, I skirted the perimeter of a park—Piazza Garibaldi—full of murmuring groups of teenagers. Just before I reached the side street by my hotel, I looked ahead and down Via T. D'Aquino, a wide boulevard barricaded against motor traffic by giant flower planters. Instead of the usual polluting cars that clog Italian city streets, people were everywhere. It was *passeggiata*, that time in the early evening when all over Italy people wander out into the public squares of their towns and villages to see and to be seen, and to catch up on the day's gossip with their neighbors.

I remembered my first *passeggiata*—or at least the first one I recall with any kind of awareness. I was in Città di Castello, a small Umbrian hill town, with my new wife and her two teenage children. We had agreed to meet in the town square at six o'clock. I was an hour early and sat on the stoop of the post office in the late afternoon sun. I must have dozed against that stone pillar because I only gradually became aware of a low murmuring, getting louder and louder. I had closed my eyes to a near-empty square. I opened them to a square filled with people, standing in small groups, talking, gesturing, patting and poking babies, laughing and linking arms with their companions.

Through this hubbub of sound, I noticed my wife walking through the square between her son and daughter, their arms linked, laughing and all speaking at once. In the midst of a cluster of Italians following a time-honored tradition—a *passeggiata*, or walkabout—of keeping solid their connections to one another, I realized I was beginning to firm up my new connections.

Another trip and several *passeggiate* later, some friends and I drove into Pistoia between the Tuscan towns of Lucca and Florence. We had been traveling all day, sight-seeing and visiting hill town after hill town. I was tired and wanted to head back to my *pensione*, but they insisted on one more stop. Amidst my grumbling, we parked in Pistoia's modern outskirts and walked a few blocks into the old town center. We rounded a corner and I heard that familiar rumble of voices and saw the streets alive with people, young and old, standing and talking. The evening was cold and threatening rain. It didn't matter. It was

A drawbridge connects Taranto's old town on the left to the new town. A medieval fort sits near the spot where a Roman garrison held off the Carthaginian general Hannibal for two years. The canal was dug in the Middle Ages, making the point of the peninsula first occupied by the Greeks in the late eighth century B.C.E. into an island. *Photo by Paul Paolicelli*

passeggiata. With friends, I forgot my fatigue and joined the masses, soaking in Italy once again.

Taranto, hundreds of miles to the south at the other end of Italy and, as far as northerners are concerned, another world away, was no different. I turned away from the direction of my hotel and plunged into the crowd along Via T. D'Aquino. It was less than two weeks before Easter. Jovial Tarantans sold, from sidewalk stands, giant, elaborately decorated chocolate eggs, a traditional *dolce*, or sweet, found all over Italy during the Easter season.

A church tucked in along a tiny square was so full of people that the crowd was overflowing down the steps and into the street. I wedged my way in and saw a procession of young

Catholic boys who appeared to be about fourteen years old, garbed head to foot in white fabric, complete with hoods and tiny holes for the eyes. Barefoot, they were making their agonizingly slow way down the church aisle, two by two, moving ahead only inches at a time, arms locked, and swaying side to side, as one.

Finally, each twosome reached the altar, where an older colleague stood with a large, body-sized crucifix. Each pair knelt before the crucified wooden figure of Christ and kissed the carved feet. Then the boys removed their masks, revealing themselves to the congregation and their proud parents, friends, and relatives: an ancient rite of passage marking the coming of age. The procession must have gone on for hours. The lineup of boys awaiting their turns at the back of the church disappeared into a side room. In the thirty minutes or so I was there, I watched only three pairs of young men make their way along the aisle.

I left to resume my personal *passeggiata* along via T. D'Aquino and stopped for a *gelato*—my evening ration of a remarkable ice cream–like Italian confection unmatched just about anywhere outside of Italy. A pretty teenaged girl, a *ragazza*, behind the counter took my order, which I offered in halting Italian. She responded in very proper English: "Where are you from in America?" I told her, in Italian. "Is it beautiful there?" she asked. I said it was. She said, "You speak excellent Italian! Your pronunciation is perfect."

"And you speak excellent English," I said, laboriously searching for the proper Italian words, knowing that her command of English was far superior to my efforts at her language.

I was in Taranto four nights. Each night I went into that shop and each time the young woman and I conversed in each other's language, together experiencing a short lesson mixed with geography.

Once she said, "I know about California. Have you been there?" I told her I had, that my grandparents had lived in a tiny beach community north of Los Angeles and, a long time ago, I would go there with my parents to visit during summer vacations.

"It seems it would be so warm and pleasant there," she said, looking, and sounding, wistful.

"But isn't it warm and pleasant here?" I asked. "People travel from all over the world to come here, and you have it all the time."

"Yes," she said, "the summers are hot, the winters, as you see, are mild. "But *California*! It is better, yes?"

"Not better, not worse. Just different," I responded.

"Perhaps," she said, showing wise insight, "it is the 'difference' I want."

Her dark eyes set in olive skin, framed by long, dark hair, and her enthusiasm for her job, life, language, and travel, reminded me of my daughter oceans away, anxious always to move on toward the different and the unexpected, no matter where she has landed.

"I leave tomorrow," I told *la ragazza*.

"See, you move on always, too."

"*Sì,*" I said.

Chapter 12

Line in the Sand

The next day sparkled under shocking blue skies. No clouds. The sea-level light was intense. The greening trees seemed greener. The washed blues of door frames seemed bluer. The air tasted delicious and I felt myself bounce with each step. I knew I was in a wonderful place.

The chill of the threatening weather of the day before was gone. I spent the morning at the archaeological digs at Metaponto south along the Gulf of Taranto shoreline. After lunch, with a clearer idea of distance and location, I set out to spend more time along the banks of the Galeso, unimpeded by a taxi's ticking meter.

I found a city bus that followed the general route my taxi driver had taken the day before. We left from the *stazione*, rumbled through Taranto's suburban streets along the north shore of the Little Sea, and sped onto the main highway cutting northeastward across Italy's heel. We crossed the bridge over the Galeso and, a mile or so farther along, the bus driver dropped me off, pointing to where I could catch a ride back.

"But hurry," he said. "You have only two hours before the final bus." En route, he had been intrigued about my desire to see the Galeso. "It is not much," he said. "Very short." I asked him if he knew about its reputation in antiquity, and he thought a moment, as if trying to remember a long-ago school lesson. "*Sì, sì.*" He laughed. "*I Greci!*"

I left the bus and walked along a narrow roadway through a decrepit warehouse district. There was some kind of naval base there, also probably a target of British bombs more than a half century earlier. *I cani liberi* lined portions of the roadway that led to the rail line just ahead. I am terrified by dogs running free. My hand unconsciously went up to where I felt the small scar under my right eye, left by a neighbor's dog that caught me by surprise when I was eight. I moved past each group gingerly. Sometimes the dogs would sit up, look at me, and, as I went by, lie down again. They didn't bark; they just watched.

Relieved and repeatedly looking over my shoulder, I reached the rail line. Then, just before crossing under the rails so I could turn left and follow a rain-puddled road to the Galeso bridge, I saw an unusual stone monument. On it were listed names with a carving of the Star of David next to each one. What appeared to be birth dates by each name ranged from 1912 to 1924, and the monument had been dedicated, out here in the countryside several miles from the city, in the mid 1960s.

It was plain, simple, and surrounded by pots that once held bright, vibrant flowers. What could it denote? Was it a marker commemorating a family of Italian Jews lost in the war? Was it in memory of a family who may have lived at the tiny farm located just off the road? Were people lined up and shot at this spot, as they had been by the Nazis in so many places in Italy?

Italy is like that: full of monuments and small remembrances, in the form of crosses by a roadside with pictures of the deceased attached or a name painted on the horizontal arm of each cross. Someday, I thought, I would return and seek out the story of this monument, beautifully carved in stone and freshened periodically with flowers.

Just across the narrow dirt road, directly opposite the marker, were the ruins of a strikingly familiar structure. It looked like an ancient way station, the kind built by the Romans every few miles or so along the various roads they carved out of the then Italian wilderness. I knew the Via Appia came through this area, but ancient geographer Strabo said it entered Tarentum a few miles away, closer to the gulf. This dirt road skirted this shore of the Little Sea in the direction of the Adriatic port city now called Bríndisi. This route matched maps I had seen showing how the Appia kissed the edge of the *Mare Piccolo*. Perhaps the road Strabo described was only an ancient "off-ramp" into the city.

Could this dirt country road cover a portion of the stone highway built by the Romans more than two thousand years ago? Just a few miles inland of where I stood was the Italian highway S7 that follows much of the original Via Appia through the mountains of modern-day Basilicata, once the Roman, and later Italian Fascist, province of Lucania. My map was not detailed enough to tell me precisely whether this dirt road is in a direct line with S7, the old Via Appia.

So many mysteries and not enough time to discover the answers! Perhaps a search for the monument's origins and the Roman road could be an excuse for another trip.

I thought about Romans and their roads. At the empire's height, these *strade* ribbed the Mediterranean world, reaching far north into England and across North Africa, spanning the entire southern shore of the Mediterranean. In all, the Romans built about fifty-three thousand miles of hard-surfaced highways made from giant paving stones, laid so they became slightly convex, or rounded up, in the middle—the origin of "high" way?—to allow rain to run off.

They were built for military reasons—a fast, easy way to move large armies into the provinces. And they were generally straight. Men walking in formation did not need gradual curves as modern vehicles do to make it across a rolling countryside.

These ancient roads were often built of concrete the Romans made from volcanic ash and lime, in addition to the large flat stones. Authoritative sources report that the Romans learned much about road building from the peoples they conquered early in their drive for empire: the Etruscans, who used cement and paved streets throughout their cities and villages before the Romans became a regional power; the Greeks, who taught Romans masonry skills; Cretans and Carthaginians, who knew how to lay down paving stones; and Egyptians and Phoenicians, who perfected the art of surveying.

The magnificent roads were carried over marshes, lakes, ravines, and mountains. The depth of the road and its base varied from three to six feet; the Via Appia one of the earliest of these roads, was thirty-five feet wide.

I crossed under the small bridge that carried rails over the dirt road, turned south, and followed along the tracks an even narrower road pocked with deep mud puddles. Within a few moments, I was under the bridge where Giuseppe said the British bomb had fallen fifty-eight years earlier.

An elderly man was walking toward me, his cane tapping the worn and battered roadway. He was slightly bent and dressed in tan pants, a light brown, well-worn sweater over a checkered shirt, and a cap—traditional, middle-aged Italian-male attire. We nodded and I struck up a conversation about the river. Did he live nearby? Did he know *il Galeso*?

"*Sì.*" And then he asked me, "Do you know that this is a very famous river?" I said I did and that I had traveled a long distance to see it. He seemed amused. "Why is it famous?" I asked, knowing the answer and anxious to hear his response. He did not disappoint me. "*I Greci,*" he said with a shrug, adding, "and the Roman poet Horace."

"*Lo conosco*" (I know him), I said.

I studied the water. Under the rail bridge, it comes up in the reeds just beyond, squeezes through a narrow concrete slot, then spreads out into a ten-foot-wide channel full of more reeds and smooth, green moss. Here, the single rows of towering trees along each bank began. If I framed the river and its banks toward where it emptied into the Little Sea a few hundred feet beyond, and eliminated the surrounding littered fields from my vision, it truly is an idyllic sight.

At our feet were swirling masses of fish of all sizes.

The old man pointed to a school and commented that the fish in this river were the best around. They are much sought after, he said. I could see why. Despite the river's location in a trashy area that is crossed, a few hundred feet apart, by a superhighway and railroad, the water appeared clean. The fish moved in and out of the moss along the river bottom.

We said good-bye. I began walking along the river to the Little Sea, and the old man headed off toward the reeds where the Galeso springs out of the ground. Ahead of me, in the distance where the tops of crab pots stuck darkly out of the water, I saw small, colorful fishing boats painted in bright blues, reds, and yellows. They were moored across the Galeso's mouth.

I could hear dogs barking and caught glimpses of them running together, back and forth along the shore. I saw a fisherman standing on a dock, untangling his nets. He looked at me and we nodded. I pointed to the dogs and asked if I was safe. He shouted at them and they immediately calmed down, backing away from me.

I walked to where the tiny river flowed into the Little Sea, took photographs, and watched the dusk settle over the water and shoreline. I looked toward the city and thought of Gissing's words, written about his few moments of sitting at this very spot: "There was a good view of Taranto across the water; the old town on its little island, compact of white houses, contrasting with the yellowish tints of the great new buildings which spread over the peninsula." This was precisely what I was seeing, standing here at dusk, the fisherman beside me working on his nets.

Gissing continues: "Far away, the boats of fishermen floated silently. I heard a rustle as an old fig tree hard by dropped its latest leaves. On the sea bank of yellow crumbling earth, lizards flashed about me in the sunshine. After a dull morning, the day had passed into golden serenity; a stillness as of eternal peace held earth and sky."

With one last look, I walked back to my bus stop, at least a mile away. As I stood there, waiting for the orange Italian bus *Numero 9*, I noticed still another pack of *i cani libri* in the distance. They were heading toward where I was standing out in the open, no cars or houses in sight. I nervously shifted from one foot to the other, glancing about and wondering where I could go, what I could do, if they attacked me. I remembered the movie *Never Cry Wolf* about a scientist studying wolves in the far north of North America. He had staked out his territory the way he had observed a male wolf do—by urinating in spots around his camp.

I looked around. No bus yet, no cars, no people. Like the scientist, I scurried from spot to spot, leaving my "mark" in a semicircle around the bus stop. Then, hands in pockets so I wouldn't appear aggressive, I waited. The dogs noticed me and started to spread out in front of me. They hit my territorial line. They stopped, sniffed, looked at me, looked at one another, and then, as if on cue, regrouped and gaily trotted off toward the Little Sea.

In a few moments, my bus, right on time, lumbered into sight.

Chapter 13

A walk in the sun

My second visit to the Galeso had followed a half-day trip to Metaponto, established by the Greeks as Metapontion and renamed Metapontum by the Romans. The village is located south along the gulf coast, and on its outskirts is the site of a Greek temple that Gissing had walked to with a young Italian boy as his guide. This ancient spot was colonized by people from Sybaris and Kroton, back in the eighth century B.C.E., when the two cities were much friendlier than they were two hundred years later. The Sybarites may have wanted to create a buffer town between their city and Taras (Taranto) to the northeast.

Metapontion was where Pythagoras, the Greek mathematician and philosopher who created a religious order, lived after he was banished from his home city of Kroton. He died in Metapontion in 498 B.C.E. His tomb, which has disappeared, reportedly was visited by the Roman orator Cicero in the first century B.C.E.

I vaguely knew the name of Pythagoras from high-school

geometry classes. But what drove him out of Kroton and exiled him to Metaponto was not his theories about triangles: "The square of the length of the hypotenuse of a right triangle equals the sum of the squares of the lengths of the other two sides." Rather, historians say he was driven out for his beliefs that reality is mathematical in nature, philosophy can be used for spiritual purification, the soul can rise to union with the divine, and that certain symbols have mystical significance.

Pythagoras created an order of followers committed to strict loyalty and secrecy. The order also got involved in politics, and that signaled its banishing to Metapontion, just a few miles inland from the Gulf of Taranto. In the middle of the fifth century B.C.E., the order was violently suppressed.

Nearly three hundred years after the death of Pythagoras, Metapontion's inhabitants, known throughout ancient history as a people whose political alliances shifted with the winds, were friendly to Hannibal. There, the Carthaginian general made the town his base for two years while laying siege to the Romans at Tarentum near the end of his sixteen-year, late-third-century-B.C.E. expedition that ran the length of the Italian peninsula—the Second Punic War. When Hannibal left Metapontion, he took the citizens with him in his retreat south to save them from the wrath of the Romans and, according to one historian, "to make use of [the city's] manpower in his wars against the [native] Bruttians."

The city's hospitality toward Rome's enemy was the beginning of the end for renamed Metapontum, which declined after the Carthaginian general—with no support from his North African homeland and increasing Roman victories—

The *Tavole Palatine*, the Tables of the Knights, was the only ruined temple Gissing saw during a day trip to Metaponto southwest of Taranto. In more recent times, a large Greek/Roman city has been uncovered near here. One hundred years ago, this temple sat abandoned in a farmer's field, overgrown with high grass and vines. Today this dog, one of the area's *cani liberi* (free-running dogs), appears to stand guard at the spot, believed dedicated to the Greek goddess Hera.
Photo by John Keahey

made his dash south to Kroton, his jumping-off point for a humiliating retreat to Africa. Cicero reports that in the first century B.C.E., Metapontum, like all the Greek cities, was in decline. By the second century C.E., "nothing remained but the town walls and the theater; the rest was completely ruined."

A century ago, Gissing did not know the location of these ruins, twenty feet or so below the farmers' fields he walked across to get to the temple, known as the *Tavole Palatine* (Tables of the Knights), the only ruin that he knew existed above the ground's surface, other than the Greek-era tombs that pepper the surrounding countryside.

There, at the then hidden site of the original Greek, and later

Roman, city, he must have walked over the top of the temple dedicated to Apollo Lycaeus, now the centerpiece of a late-twentieth-century archaeological exploration. Today, only that temple's foundations remain in place. Archaeologists have erected some columns to show how some of the surrounding buildings might have looked, including a portion of an amphitheater, but the site still has much to reveal to modern eyes.

The *parco archeologico* was expanded during 1998. An area immediately to the south of the original dig has been fenced off along the approaching roadway, and some earth scraped away to prepare the land for careful excavation, which is expected to take place as the twentieth century draws to a close.

This is an area revealed by the careful study of the aerial photographs first presented by the British to the Italians after World War II. The photographs had been taken to guide British planes for bombing runs in 1943, just before the Italians surrendered and the Germans occupied Italy. Similar photographs surely pinpointed for British bombers the rail line over Gissing's beloved Galeso.

Photographs taken over Metaponto and other areas in southern Italy have proved invaluable to Italian archaeology, showing the outlines of ancient cities buried just under the surface and impossible to see at ground level.

"The result of this gift [from the British] was fantastic," Professor Baldassare Conticello says. "They [the photos] were born out of violence and now are used for a greater good."

Gissing, one hundred years before my visit, saw only the city's second temple, the Tavole Palatine. It came to be known by that name during the Saracen wars that swept through this fertile area in the ninth and tenth centuries C.E. Built in the sixth century B.C.E.—with several of its original thirty-two Doric columns still standing—it is located a few miles to the northwest of the old city's center and hard against the south bank of the Bradano River.

Now, S106, the main north–south road along the Ionian coast, slips past the east edge of the site, giving motorists a dramatic view of this massive structure. Many believe the temple was dedicated to the Greek goddess Hera, wife of the mythical Zeus. The only clue that this was her temple was the inscription beginning "Hera . . ." found on a potsherd uncovered adjacent to it.

S106 did not exist in Gissing's time. The temple simply sat in the middle of a farmer's field, surrounded by a ten-foot-high wall "so that any view of [the columns] is no longer obtainable." The lock "that has long been useless" failed to keep the gate closed, so "the ugly wall serves no purpose whatever save to detract from the beauty of the scene."

He approached the site with a young guide via a "cart road, through fields just being ploughed for grain. . . . Ploughing was a fit sight at Metapontum, famous of old for the richness of its soil." After the city was abandoned, the shore here became infested with malarial swamps, making it "too dangerous for habitation. Of all the cities upon the Ionian Sea, only Tarentum and [K]roton continued to exist through the Middle Ages, for they alone occupied a position strong for defence against pirates and invaders."

Gissing despaired at the temple's condition, and at how many of the huge stone blocks that once completed the religious center had been hauled away over intervening centuries for use elsewhere.

Today, I believe, he would be pleased with what has happened here. While what Gissing saw then is what people can see today—the same upright columns—the nineteenth-century farmer's field has been transformed into a *parco* around the impressive Greek temple. There is no trace of the ugly wall. A tiny museum sits at the entrance, and the grounds are like a garden, the pride of the region's tourist industry.

The present-day village of Metaponto also has another museum, this one brand-new in the late 1990s. I was eager to see it.

I climbed off the train, probably at the same Metaponto *stazione* from which Gissing disembarked—it was old and battered, with peeling, lemon yellow paint, looking as if it had withstood at least a dozen or more decades of use and weather. I walked a half mile into the modern village. The proprietor of a coffee bar gave me directions to the new museum, a few blocks away. *"É bello!"* she said of the new structure, her eyes and smile demonstrating the pride she felt for her town and its prize.

I was the *museo's* only patron at that moment. A curator greeted me and enthusiastically answered my halting questions, asked in poor Italian, about excavations in the area. He guided me through all the rooms, speaking his language and southern dialect so rapidly and excitedly that I couldn't keep up.

The museum displays artifacts from the Apollo Lycaeus dig a few miles north of the museum, and from the tombs unearthed on the museum grounds—the unmarked tomb of Pythagoras?—and elsewhere throughout the area: pottery, tools, jewelry.

The curator unlocked one room, showing me a series of aerial photographs of the area, one set taken in 1943 by British bombers and another taken in 1973. From one to the other, I could see the hidden ruins slowly emerging from where they had been secreted twenty feet below the fields across which the unaware Gissing trudged.

I left the museum and walked, in the warm Italian sun, the one or two miles along a narrow country road to the archaeological park and what has been identified as the Sanctuary of Apollo Lycaeus. The route was through land rapidly turning green and full of those yellow wildflowers, patches sprinkled occasionally with reds and blues. It was classic Italian-spring scenery: a series of wonderful stone farm buildings, some modern, some crumbling and overrun with vines.

The Apollo Lycaeus site, with its columnless temple, was marked at the far end by rows of temporary low-slung wooden warehouses full of artifacts unearthed from the ancient city. Workers were busy cataloging pottery and pieces of columns and capitals. It was a supermarket of structures, row upon row, inside the buildings, along the porches and out in the courtyard. There was no admission fee and no guidebook—a true archaeological work-in-progress.

Many of the treasures of Metaponto can be found in the archaeological museum in Taranto. This large nineteenth-century structure is located in the new city, south of the drawbridge, and is, I believe, the very museum Gissing walked through near the end of his visit here.

On my final morning in Italy's heel, after my usual *cornetto* and *caffè doppio*, I walked the few blocks from my hotel to the museum, which contained by far the most extensive collection of Greek and Roman pottery I had come across. Not only were there numerous examples of the different periods in its evolution, but much of it was intact. It is amazing to see a giant vase, done in the Hellenistic period so many thousands of years ago, in its original wholeness.

I was disappointed that a visitor was not guided, by the museum's floor plan, through successive periods of time. The prehistoric material from the ancient Italic tribes native to the region was on a different, higher, floor. And the Greek and Roman materials are not displayed in order of their progression, say, from archaic to Hellenic. Other museums establish this progression well, like the displays do in, for example, Síbari, farther to the south, or at Siracusa on the southeast coast of Sicily.

On this day, I was lucky. Just like Gissing, I had the museum to myself. It was just the guards and me. I spent three or four hours combing the displays. I heard only the footsteps of passing guards and museum personnel, rushing past without a glance at the displays I lingered over, their leather shoes clicking against the tile floor and the sound bouncing off the fifteen-or-twenty-foot-high walls.

It was almost as if nothing had changed in this display area over the intervening century. What Gissing described, I saw.

"Upon the shelves are seen innumerabble [sic] busts, carved in some kind of stone; thought to be simply portraits of private persons. One peers into the faces of men, women and children, vaguely conjecturing their date, their circumstances; some of them may have dwelt in the old time on this very spot of ground now covered by the Museum."

Rereading that passage just before entering the museum, I was struck by how much alike Gissing and I thought. Since childhood, I would go someplace historic and imagine stepping on the ground in the very places historic people had stepped. As an adult, I put my hand on a banister in George Washington's home at Mount Vernon, Virginia, wondering if his hand had ever rested on that very spot. I stood beneath the Arch of Titus in the Roman forum, wondering if Titus, who had made his name by the destruction of Jerusalem, had ever walked on the stones on which I was standing.

Another time, a friend in Rome told me he had once attended a reception at the Palazzo Venezia. Mussolini had stood on a small, narrow balcony of this palace, looking over the chanting and cheering million or so souls jammed into the piazza below. Today, the piazza is full of cars more often than cheering crowds, although politicians often hold rallies there. Across from the balcony on the piazza below where it connects with the head of the famous Corso, stands a beautifully uniformed traffic cop on a small round platform, his—and sometimes her—white-gloved hands orchestrating the movements of thousands of automobiles per hour.

My friend said he looked out through the draped windows leading onto Mussolini's balcony and searched for the likely spot where he thought Mussolini must have stood. He could hear the jarring maelstrom of traffic below. I wish I could have seen that sight and stood in the spot where Mussolini, his jutting jaw and head bobbing up and down as he received the crowd's adoration, was portrayed in newsreel after newsreel.

So, once again, I found myself walking across a floor in a museum that a Victorian writer, and who knows who else, once trod upon.

Sound did carry in this museum! As I rounded the second turn on the floor containing the most magnificent Greek pieces, I could hear loud talking at the far end. A group of custodians and guards were engrossed in loud banter—the kind that visitors to Italy often mistake for arguing; in reality, it is only passionate discussion among members of a passionate culture. It is charming to watch such intense conversation in cafés or on the street corner, but not in a museum.

I selfishly wanted my uninterrupted privacy to look at the objects and reflect on who made them and how they were made. Day after day, workers in such a museum could become oblivious to the antiquity surrounding them; I had a few hours left here and did not want to be so distracted, as I had once been in Florence. This had been in the late 1980s, and I had wandered into a museum—I do not remember where it was—but it housed wonderful bronze statues and marvelous paintings. The room was nearly empty—I seem to luck into uncrowded places—and the staff was at the end having a heated discussion, Italian style. The noise was unbearable and I had no phrase book or knowledge of the language to help me. I simply left after only a few moments, unable to stand the intensity of the Great Debate at the end of the room.

This time, though, I was not deterred. Consulting my pocket Italian-English dictionary, I walked to the end of the room where the cluster of three or four museum personnel gathered around a tiny desk, gesturing at one another, talking rapidly and loudly about the latest state lottery and what each would do if he or she was the winner. I stood there a moment. They noticed me, and the snatches of conversation drifted off. In my most reasonable voice I said: *"Mi scusate. Taciate, per favore"* (Excuse me. Please, be quiet). Instantly, the group fell silent. The woman sitting at the desk looked sincerely apologetic and said, *"Sì. Scusi, signore."*

From then on, for most of the next hour I was in the area,

this group huddled closer together, speaking in excited, very low stage whispers. Occasionally one voice would grow loud, and I would hear a quick series of shushes and the conversation level would drop once again. As I left the room, I could hear their voices rising. No visitor was in the room behind me. The workers once again had it all to themselves.

I was at the end of my visit in Taranto—this charming city high on the inside of Italy's heel. Like Gissing, I had seen the Galeso and trudged the picturesque road to the digs at Metaponto. I had been circled by dogs and held them off—an experience Gissing did not mention—and had walked through the old city, still with its medieval structures built on top of Roman and Greek foundations.

Taranto's only problem as far as drawing greater numbers of tourists is that it is isolated in the far South, well out of the way of the North's larger tourist appeal, and therefore it is often bypassed. A pity. This land is dotted with palm trees and its cities are as old as recorded time itself. Perhaps, for the selfish, occasional visitor, this isolation from mainstream tourism is not so bad after all.

A few hours after visiting the museum, I walked back to the train station, thinking about the next major town on my Gissing agenda: Crotone. From this city, then called Kroton, Hannibal embarked for Carthage in North Africa, near modern Tunis and just across the Ionian Sea from Sicily, where the Ionian once again becomes the Mediterranean. He left in shame after sixteen years in Italy, ultimately failing to defeat Rome.

Some ancient writings suggest it was on the beaches near today's Crotone—beaches where locals and tourists walk their dogs and play soccer—that before climbing into their boats,

A Sweet and Glorious Land

Hannibal's men slaughtered four thousand native Italian mercenaries who had loyally fought with him against the Romans but,
not wanting to leave their homeland, refused the Carthaginian's
offer to take them with him to a strange and foreign land.

Chapter 14

The Albergo Concordia

Leaving Taranto, the train crosses through rolling, sandy hills marked by short, stubby pines. The ground, in more open places, is carpeted with various low-lying wildflowers: the yellows I had seen earlier through the Crati valley, and others, a pink, delicate color, blooming heavily in the Ionian sun.

We crossed many rivers and streams, emptying their load from Basilicata's mountainous slopes into the Gulf of Taranto. These are many of the waterways that attracted the Greeks to this shoreline's fertile soils. Some of the streams are broad and smooth, lined by short stalks of dry reeds. Others are captured in concrete troughs, like the Busento and Crati just before they sweep past Cosenza, deeper inland.

All along the rail line grows flat-bladed cactus, some spiky, like sabers, others smooth and curved like thick slices of ham. Just as the terms for changes in weather mystify me, I have woefully inadequate knowledge about the plants I see. I do not even remember the names for many that I have planted deep into the rich, dark soil of my garden back home. Gissing knew the names of much of what he saw here, a habit he picked up from his voracious reading and his long, solitary walks back in his English home.

The shoreline speeding past my compartment window is not as sparse as it was in Gissing's time, ten decades earlier. All along the gulf's coast are little twentieth-century towns, marinas, and what appear to be summer homes and resorts. After Metaponto but before Marina di Ginosa, the land flattens out, perfect for farming. As we move farther inland, the land reminds me of the fertile Snake River plain of my childhood home in Idaho.

But in this very South of Italy, sweeping, curving, tiny marsh-lined rivers run through orange and lemon groves. It is early spring, but I see acres of land that are also filled with vegetables and grain. Some fields lie fallow. I wonder what rests twenty feet below these fields—ancient temples, columns, and stone burial vaults?

Past the train *stazione* at the tiny hamlet of Policoro-Tursi, I begin to see foothills to the northwest. Hill towns dot the tops of their brown promontories. We are still inland, but should move closer to the shore after we cross from Basilicata into Calabria. In a few moments, my train will reach Síbari, where Gissing lunched only a few miles from the then hidden ruins of what many believe are the Greek cities of Sybaris and Thurii, one on top of the other, and then, built over the same spot from the rubble of the first two, the Roman city of Copia. That which Gissing did unknowingly I do knowingly, riding the rails past the archaeological site that had to wait until the mid-twentieth century to begin yielding its wealth of ancient history.

Gissing's days in Crotone were perhaps his most introspective and spiritual, probably because of the intensity of his sickness and his fevered inability to get to his goal: the single column of a ruined Greek temple to Hera at Capo Colonna. He spent ten days there and many were passed in bed, lying on sweat-soaked sheets, burning with fever and hallucinating about life in these ancient colonies.

He knew the town, facing the Ionian Sea on the southwest coast of southern Italy, by the name of Cotrone, the name dating back to the Middle Ages. It was not changed to the modern, more Greek-like spelling—Crotone, based on the original Greek name Kroton—until 1928, some thirty years after his visit. I knew that the squalid hotel he had stayed in, the Concordia, no longer existed in name. But I wanted to find where it had been and see what was there now: an office for a lawyer, perhaps, or a new Standa, the Italian version of the American department store.

The Greeks founded Kroton about 710 B.C.E., a decade after Sybaris and only a year or two before Taras, both to the north. Like Sybaris, it was in its glory only a few hundred years. But instead of being washed away like Sybaris or abandoned as were successor cities Thurii and Copia, ancient Kroton simply evolved over successive generations, and the site has been in constant use.

A short time after the Krotonians destroyed Sybaris, about 510 B.C.E., they in turn were defeated by Greeks from Syrakusai, modern Siracusa in Sicily, as well as native tribes, foreign invaders, and finally the Romans. Later came the Normans, Saracens, and many others. Some of the city's conquerors were, over the previous centuries, from cities that were former allies. This was an era when Greeks, united all over the southern Mediterranean by cultural similarities, were still divided because they owed their first allegiance to their individual cities, which were in effect individual states.

As on the Greek mainland for hundreds of years, city battled city over the smallest of slights. For example, the Krotonians believed the Sybarites were too luxury-loving and did not have the respect for temples and religious traditions those in Kroton thought they should; hence, their battles.

This idea of city opposing city was carried into medieval Italy as well, a time when city-states such as Florence battled for supremacy with towns such as Siena during the Renaissance. It was not civil war when one city fought another. It was more like international warfare—the same as when the Germanic tribes invaded Gaul or the Romans landed along England's southern coast.

Italians first claim allegiance to families, then their neighborhoods, their cities of birth, their province and region and, finally, the "nation"—but only if the national soccer team happens to be in the World Cup. *Italian* is a word that describes cultural state of mind long before it denotes political boundaries. Sicilians, for example, are Siracusans first, then Sicilians, and last, perhaps, Italians.

Modern-day Crotone, its nondescript stuccoed buildings spreading up a promontory, sits jutting into an azure sea at the point below where the Gulf of Taranto to the northeast ends and the Ionian Sea once again caresses Italy's sole. The *città vecchia*, with much more character than the *città nuova*, tops the promontory and is dominated by the remains of a crumbling medieval castle dating back to the early 1500s C.E. That castle, or what is left of it, sits where the first Greek acropolis was built shortly after the city was established. Nothing of that original structure remains above ground. The remains of the Greek temple Gissing sought, with its single shattered column, was ten miles to the south.

Ancient writers say Kroton's city walls ultimately reached

twelve miles in length, much greater than the walls of Sybaris, which were only five and a half miles in circumference at the time of that city's destruction.

Up by the castle and across the narrow street sit medieval houses and seventeenth- and eighteenth-century *palazzi*, made from the stones pilfered from those crumbling Greek, and, later, Roman temples and walls. It was from beaches south of here, out along the promontory of Capo Colonna, that the Carthaginian general Hannibal set sail after his failed sixteen-year war against the Romans. Those beaches—if early Roman writers can be believed—were left bloody and heaped with the bodies of native Italian mercenaries who had refused to go along with Hannibal in his humiliating retreat to North Africa. Fearing that those mercenaries would someday be hired to fight against him on another battlefield, he took no chances.

One hundred years ago the town of Cotrone ended just a short walk beyond the square outside Gissing's hotel window. He walked along the northernmost of three town roads that move away from the square, like spokes from a hub, toward the Esaro River. His road, then as now, was the main street into town from the train station. "Bordered on both sides by warehouses of singular appearance," the road led to a bridge and to the plentiful orange groves along the river's banks—now replaced by buildings of an ugly industrial quarter. Those warehouses are still there, but instead of storing grain, they house a series of auto-repair shops and car dealerships.

This Esaro, which flows into the Ionian Sea near the town's center, is a different river from the Esaro that shares with the Crati the valley on the other side of Grand Sila mountain to the north. That was the valley I had traversed en route to the Ionian coastline after I left Cosenza several days earlier.

A Sweet and Glorious Land

In Crotone, rock-hard sand hills streaked with gullies and speckled with low-growing green shrubs now, as in Gissing's day, provide a backdrop to the town's southwest quarter. But the spit of land between the hills and the beach of Crotone's tiny southeast bay has filled up over the past century with hotels, apartment houses, and, of course, automobiles.

Near this area, along the road that skirts these beaches and modern buildings, sits a tiny, high-walled cemetery that must have been here for hundreds of years. The entrance marks the spot where the town's road ended in the late 1890s. Only a narrow trail continued on in those days toward Capo Colonna, Gissing's unrealized destination, where the single column rises out of the much-abused remains of the twenty-seven-hundred-year-old Greek temple to Hera.

Gissing visited the well-kept cemetery and spent time talking to its aged caretaker, who had planted trees, shrubs, and flowers to maintain a place of beauty. Unfortunately, Gissing does not give us the name of this gentleman, whose story evokes a longing in the reader to know him better. "When I took leave, the kindly fellow gave me a large bunch of flowers, carefully culled, with many regrets that the lateness of the season forbade his offering choicer blossoms. His simple good nature and intelligence greatly won upon me. I like to think of him as still quietly happy amid his garden walls, tending flowers that grow over the dead at Cotrone."

More than a decade after Gissing, Scottish writer Norman Douglas visited the same cemetery, hoping to talk to the caretaker his compatriot had written about. Alas, Douglas discovered the old man had died: "Dead, like those whose graves he tended; like Gissing himself. [The old man] expired in February 1901—the year of the publication of the *Ionian Sea*, and they showed me his tomb near the right side of the entrance; a poor little grave, with a wooden cross bearing a number, which will soon be removed to make room for another one." Sadly, Douglas does not give us the caretaker's name either.

Today, as Douglas predicted would happen, there is no sign of that caretaker's niche. I walked through the cemetery, looked to the right of the entrance, and discovered that all the old graves and tombs I saw dated back only to the first decades of the 1900s, principally the 1920s through modern times. No one from 1901 was there. I have heard that it is a tradition in Italian cemeteries to remove bones from older graves, store them in special boxes in musty crypts, and then fill the newly vacated grave sites with the more recently deceased. This must be the case here as the sacred ground is disturbed over and over, generation after generation.

Today, a paved road continues south from the cemetery entrance, running along the beach in front and leading to a point ten miles away where Hera's column rises out of the boulder-strewn land. To get to Capo Colonna one hundred years ago, Gissing would have had to ride a donkey along a narrow dirt path that extended beyond the cemetery, or take a boat, as most townspeople did, across the choppy bay to the remote point jutting out into the blue Ionian.

He never made it. The wind was too strong for small boats during his first few days at the Concordia. Then sickness took over, and Gissing spent much of his remaining time confined to his tiny room, delirious and under a doctor's care.

Chapter 15

Pictures on a Wall

When I arrived a little more than one hundred years to the day after Gissing was here, the Concordia had been gone for so long that no one I spoke with had ever heard of it: the taxi driver, the waiter at a restaurant, the man in the newspaper stand near the town's square. *"Non lo so"* (I don't know), they all said.

The taxi driver told me there were two hotels in the old town's center: the Italia and the Capitol. The Italia was a single-star *pensione*. Nice, he said. Clean. The Capitol, even while undergoing renovation, was more luxurious, *tre stelle*. My budget did not include three stars, so he dropped me off in front of the Italia. I started up the stone steps toward the first level, then stopped.

Despite concerns about my budget, money was holding up well. I had stayed in a series of low-cost accommodations on this tightly financed trip. I turned around and walked down into the street, headed toward the *duomo* (cathedral), and then turned left toward the Capitol. The room there was reasonable:

about the same price I would pay in Rome for a two-star, or even my usual one-star *pensione*. Not bad, I thought. Television. A private bathroom. The irony of this choice was to play itself out the following morning.

I got up, ate the requisite hard roll and drank two cups of stony black, wonderfully bitter coffee, and set out to see if I could find the location of the old Concordia. I again talked to people on the street. They had not heard of it. I asked at a religious bookstore adjacent to the *duomo*. Same story. Soon I found myself at the crumbling castle that my guidebook said had been enlarged by a gentleman named Pietro of Toledo. It had been partially restored, and it housed, on its top rampart, a small museum.

A young boy, about fourteen with black hair framing black eyes set solidly in an olive-colored, angular face, and wearing a crisp white shirt, dark pants, and highly polished shoes, greeted me and politely asked me to sign the guest register. Looking at my signature and hometown, he marveled to a smaller, younger friend sitting nearby that here was a visitor from some place other than Italy. I was the first name in the register that morning. Only a couple of names were on the page for the preceding day.

The small two-room collection had a handful of artifacts unearthed from nearby ancient sites. But the biggest part of the collection was made up of a series of photographs of old Cotrone, mostly taken before 1928 when the town's name was slightly changed to reflect its Greek, rather than Roman, heritage.

It struck me that I might see the hotel's name in an old photo. Then, seconds after that thought, there it was: a photograph, printed in brownish sepia tones, of a doorway and the sign ALBERGO CONCORDIA on a wall next to a flight of familiar-

Gissing occupied one of the rooms of the old Albergo Concordia located above the columns in the center of this Calabrian city, known during his visit as Cotrone. The name over the doorway has changed to the Albergo Italia, and the town, in 1928, was renamed Crotone to more closely resemble the ancient Greek name of Kroton. This is where he lay sick, for nearly ten days, treated by Dr. Sculco. Here is where Lenormant, the French archaeologist, stayed a decade before Gissing, and where Norman Douglas, a Scottish writer following Gissing's Calabrian trail, stayed a little more than a decade after Gissing's 1897 visit. *Photo by John Keahey*

looking stone steps. I called the young boy over and asked him where this building was. Near the *duomo*, he said, just before the main square.

He gave me directions, hurriedly sketched on the back of an old paper scrap he scooped up from the floor. I walked down the narrow streets from the old fortress into the town center, past the *duomo*. I glanced up at the familiar building before me. The Concordia sign that had been painted at the stairwell's entrance was no longer there, of course. But higher up, bolted to the ancient stone facade, a new sign said ALBERGO ITALIA, the place I had turned my back on the previous day for more luxurious digs at the three-star Capitol!

This time, I completed the walk up the steps and into the lobby. It was silent inside—no clerk in sight—and decorated with soft, pillow-filled couches. The lobby and hallways were laid out just as Gissing described. I looked along the corridor leading to a series of rooms with a view over the square, from where Gissing once had heard the shouts of peasants loudly demonstrating against some injustice. Any one of those rooms—where he spent feverish days and nights, tended to by the literate Dr. Riccardo Sculco—could have been his.

Reading Gissing's published account of his illness in Cotrone, I got the impression that he had fondly remembered the good doctor, except when Sculco insisted that his patient remain in Cotrone to recover fully rather than head for the loftier heights of Catanzaro where the air was brisk and free of malaria. In his diaries, Gissing even referred to the doctor as "an excellent fellow," according to the editors' notes accompanying memoirs of a Gissing acquaintance, published in early 1999. The memoirs (*With Gissing in Italy: The Memoirs of Brian Ború Dunne*) are the recollections of a young American journalist who knew Gissing first in Siena and later in Rome, before and after the Englishman's Ionian trip.

Dunne remembers Gissing complaining, just weeks after the Cotrone experience, about the doctor and his methods of treatment. He called Sculco "that fool" for ordering Gissing to eat beefsteak while in a high fever, something the often sick Gissing knew better than to do. Later, Gissing told Dunne that Sculco was "that numbskull," who, later, when the patient most needed to regain strength, then refused Gissing any food: "As Gissing, thanks to nature, climbed out of the fever and began to ascend the ladder of health, the doctor exclaimed with a magnificent gesture: 'No food, *Signor*,'" Dunne reports.

From my vantage point in the Italia/Concordia hallway, I could only imagine such conversations. I looked behind me, back toward the far wall of the pleasant hotel lobby. On it hung a glass-framed page from a local newspaper, describing how in recent times the Italia took over the space once occupied by the historic Concordia—where the "British poet" Gissing once recovered from a serious illness; where the French writer Lenormant, whose journey Gissing was following, had stayed a decade before the Englishman; and where a Scottish writer, Douglas, had overnighted in the early 1900s while following a portion of Gissing's trail.

"The shade of George Gissing haunts these chambers and passages," writes Douglas of the Concordia, in his seminal work on southern Italy, *Old Calabria*, first published in 1915. Gissing had been disturbed by the squalor of the place and the bad food. Roughly fifteen years later, Douglas found a much-changed place: "The food is good and varied, the charges moderate; the place is spotlessly clean in every part. . . . 'One cannot live without cleanliness,' as the housemaid, assiduously scrubbing, remarked to me."

All the people from Gissing's Cotrone, except for Dr. Sculco, were dead when Douglas arrived: the mayor whose written permission Gissing sought to allow him to visit the orange groves along the Esaro River; the housemaid who would occasionally look in on him; the "domestic serf with dark and flashing eyes," and the hostess of 1897, "the stout, slatternly, sleepy woman who seemed surprised at my [Gissing's] demand for food, but at length complied with it."

Douglas spoke with the good doctor, who remembered his patient. "I remember him quite well; the young English poet who was quite ill here. I prescribed for him. Yes-yes! He wore his hair long," Douglas quoted Dr. Sculco, who had been only four years older than Gissing. The doctor was unwilling to say more about his long-haired charge. Douglas surmised that Sculco was following his oath never to reveal anything about patients, alive or dead.

Now here I was, several decades after Dr. Sculco and Douglas each had gone to their rest: Sculco, who died in 1931 at age seventy-six, likely buried in the city cemetery Gissing once visited; and Douglas, who, a suicide in 1952 at age eighty-three, went to his grave on Capri, off the coast of Naples. I stood in the Italia/Concordia one hundred years and approximately three months after Gissing paced this very hallway—one hundred ten years after François Lenormant passed along the street outside on donkey-back and stayed here while researching his masterwork *La Grande-Grèce: Paysages et Histoire*, the definitive late-nineteenth-century work study of Greek archaeological sites in southern Italy, and eighty-some years after Norman Douglas came via train to follow his fellow Brit's footsteps and write his own book about this region of southern Italy—a travel classic equal to Gissing's *By the Ionian Sea*.

At this moment I realized that my journey was part of a continuing trek connected to three people, much better read and steeped in the classics than I, but who shared my passion for Italy's South and for its colonial Greek heritage. The native Italic peoples, the Greeks, the Romans, Hannibal, the Saracens, the Normans, the Spanish, and other conquerors had laid out the geographic road map that we four, sharing this spot of floor in an old hotel, followed, each in our own era and with our unique perspective.

Now if I could just get to Capo Colonna and see what Gissing, gazing longingly across the bay at, failed to see up close because of growing illness: the remaining Doric column of a temple dedicated to Hera. The writer's caretaker, Dr. Sculco, had told his patient how he, as a schoolboy, would walk around and around the column near his parents' summer home, reciting out loud portions of classic literature he was memorizing.

Chapter 16

Bunkers, a Church with No Floor, a Lonely Column

The cylindrical concrete structure—a bleak, lichen-covered sentinel rooted in place for decades—greeted me as I entered Capo Colonna, the grounds just ten miles south of Crotone that hold Hera's column. I had seen, along the mountain road days earlier between Paola and Cosenza, an identical small building, also with its slotted windows wider inside than out, in a manner designed to discourage bullets and grenades from finding their way to the interior.

This mottled gray German bunker looked out from its perch over Crotone's tiny harbor, still waiting for an invasion that never came. Instead of pouring into Italy from southern Italy's Ionian coast, the Allies in 1943 invaded halfway up the peninsula—first the British at Reggio, then Americans and British at Salerno, then Anzio, both along the Tyrrhenian Sea. Today the machine-gun portals of this tiny bunker, barely big enough for two men, look across the small bay of Crotone to where joggers and dog-walkers meander.

It is always chilling to see these rounded bunkers. The first I had ever seen were in southern Sicily during a trip in 1986. I had climbed up through a farmer's field to stand on the dome, laughing and joking with a friend, until it occurred to me, looking across a small valley at similar bunkers on the other side, that from these portals blazed machine-gun fire that cut down American and British troops who came not as conquerors, but as liberators.

This bunker's open entrance, fixed on the land side of the harbor, looks in the direction of Hera's column, which rises out of the point of the cape (Capo Colonna), just a few feet from the sea.

I turned back and looked across the choppy water at the old town, today just a shimmer in the distance. I could barely make out the castle rampart where Gissing, and I, had stood a century apart. This day was frightfully, unseasonably, cold and windy, perhaps about the same as it was when he was here in late 1897. I wouldn't want to be in a boat threading my way through the raucous whitecaps. The road from the town, while narrow, was gentle and undulating. Arriving by automobile is much preferable in weather like this.

I turned around and gazed back toward the cape. Two-story houses blocked my view of the column from the German bunker. Could one of those houses—empty in winter and surrounded by high walls that also enclose growling, barking guard dogs—be the one in which Gissing's Dr. Sculco spent his youthful summers, memorizing lines from classical literature?

To the north of these homes stood a small church. It did not appear old, but it had been well maintained, and its age was difficult to determine. The front doors stood wide open. A man pushing a wheelbarrow along a plank came out of the door.

The wheelbarrow was loaded with rich, dark soil destined for a growing pile a few feet from the entrance.

I looked inside. The once-tiled floor of the tiny chapel was gone. Pieces of tile poked out of the growing mound of dirt outside. People were midway into the open space where heavy sheets of plastic covered portions of the dirt floor not being worked on. Workers were on their knees, scraping soil with small trowels. Their presence there became obvious: It was not a renovation but an archaeological dig.

I walked inside, using a long, sloping wooden ramp. Stop! a young man, obviously in charge, said in a loud voice. Everyone looked up, including the middle-aged priest who was wrapped in a black cloak and standing on a sheet of plastic, puffing on a cigarette. *"Non è permesso!"* the young man said. *"Archeologia?"* I asked. *"Sì,"* he responded abruptly, turning back to his work. I watched for a minute longer and walked back up the plank and out of the door just in time to see a passerby pull a piece of tile from the pile of dirt and tuck it into his coat pocket.

A short distance from the church, around the approaches to the two or three large stone summer homes, I found the fenced-in area surrounding Hera's column, the single remaining surface remnant of a temple that originally contained forty-eight columns. This temple was originally established in the fifth century B.C.E. Not much has been excavated here in modern times. Now all that is protected is the single column itself, its base reinforced by modern brick footings.

The grass-covered area where the once intact temple stood, once the most splendid Doric temple in southern Italy, is accessible, and though it is fenced in, there is nothing to see on the surface there except dirt paths crisscrossing through the grass.

This lonely sentinel, with the Ionian Sea in the background, is all that remains of Hera's temple at Capo Colonna, ten miles south of Crotone. Gissing longed to see this shattered Doric column, but never made it here. This is near the spot where Hannibal departed Italy to return to North Africa after failing to defeat the Romans. It is the site where his troops allegedly slaughtered four thousand native mercenaries who fought with Hannibal but who did not want to accompany him to Carthage.
Photo by John Keahey

The temple reportedly had a sculptured marble frieze, and its roof was layered in white marble, or so the ancient writers tell us. Supposedly, there was a gold column inside, along with a painting of Helen of Troy painted from a model chosen from among the fair female residents of Kroton.

The single column is a lonely sight. It and its base must be nearly all that remains of the massive structure that, over the centuries, was torn apart, stone by stone, and used to build palazzi for the rich in old Cotrone and perhaps to reinforce Pietro of Toledo's Renaissance castle. Gissing knew this, and he muttered in print about such folks who would despoil ancient sites for their own building blocks.

I wondered how long the column would stand, without further intervention from humans. To see archaeological work at the church was heartening. All over the South there seems to be a resurgence in work of this sort at many ancient sites. But not much has been done in the area of Hera's temple here. Except for a few modern buildings, the paved road, and the fence enclosing the site, the Capo Colonna must look about the same as it did one hundred, or even two hundred, years ago.

And I wonder if the sea has been rising here over the centuries. At Sybaris, farther to the north, the shoreline, built up by alluvial deposits that filled in the ancient harbor, has moved away from the ancient city. Here at Capo Colonna, the Ionian is lapping to within ten or fifteen feet of the single column's brick-reinforced base. Would the ancient Greeks have built such a temple so close to the water? A heavy storm from the southeast could dash against the column and undermine it.

But the column has indeed stood for centuries, despite raging tempests and people's best efforts at destruction. Its enemy has not been the sea, but the wealthy Cotronians who hauled away the temple's massive stones in an orgy of barbaric recycling of ready-made, and free-for-the-taking, building stones.

Since reading Gissing's work, I had always been bothered by his obsessive melancholy, expressed both in his *By the Ionian Sea* and in most of his fiction. For the first time, here at Capo Colonna with the cold wind blowing across the fluted column, I could feel some sympathy for his despair over how the modern world has turned its back on the ancient.

Sitting at its base, my back to the sea, I looked once more

around the temple enclosure. It could have been on this very spot that Hannibal sat, agonizing in his disappointment and humiliation at being forced to retreat to Carthage after nearly two decades of wreaking death and destruction on the Romans and on his own men. I wondered how many of those who started with him on that long winter journey across the Alps sixteen years earlier were still with him at the end. Damn few, probably.

Hannibal's rage against the Romans dipped back into his childhood as he watched his father, Hamilcar Barca, devastated by Roman demands to abandon Sicily at the end of the First Punic War. Carthage and Rome, once allies, were struggling to fill the vacuum of power throughout the Mediterranean created by the death of Alexander the Great, a century earlier.

Hamilcar took his son to Spain to rebuild Carthage's empire. Hannibal took over the army at his father's untimely death, fought for a few years against native Spanish tribes, and then besieged Roman ally Saguntum (now Sagunto, sixteen miles north of Valencia in Spain). Hannibal knew that act would provoke war with his father's longtime enemy.

So, in 218 B.C.E., Hannibal assembled ninety thousand men, twelve thousand horses, and thirty-seven elephants, moved west-to-east through southern France, and eventually crossed the Alps, invading Italy and catching the Romans by surprise. It was at a heavy cost. He crossed the Alps, in winter, in fifteen days, and at a considerable loss of life.

After a handful of victories and an especially decisive battle at Cannae, in southeast Italy about five and a half miles southwest of modern Barletta on the Adriatic coast, he won the military support of many cities in the South for his cause against the Romans.

But the Roman army played a waiting game, and the years passed. Hannibal once got to the gates of Rome, but unlike Alaric six centuries later, mysteriously retreated back to the South. The ancient writers tell us that one of Hannibal's generals bitterly remarked during that retreat that the Carthaginian knew how to win a battle but did not know how to win a war.

The North African general was pressed farther and farther south. On the deaths of key officers, and without hope of reinforcements from North Africa, Hannibal left the peninsula. He had spent sixteen years in Italy, living off the land, trying to break the will of Rome's allies, and terrifying Roman citizens in the Eternal City, who many times believed all was lost.

His goal was to weaken Rome to the point where Carthage would be given Sicily, Sardinia, and Corsica. But despite being recognized as one of the greatest military leaders in history, he was too far away from home fighting a war unpopular among his countrymen, and he did not sustain the support of possible European allies, including the Gauls.

Livy, the Roman historian who lived two centuries after Rome's war with Hannibal, wrote in his ten-book history of the Second Punic War that "Hannibal has been conquered not by the Roman people whom he defeated so many times in battle and put to flight, but by the envy and continual disparagement of the Carthaginian senate."

Roman propagandists painted Hannibal as bloodthirsty and cruel. Stories of his brutality against soldiers and prisoners abound. Many of the reports likely are true, since these were indeed cruel and savage times. But, as *The Oxford Classical Dictionary* puts it, "The record of Rome's treatment of defectors [the peoples and the cities that allied with Hannibal] makes for grimmer reading."

Hannibal died, in 182 B.C.E., drinking poison as enemy soldiers closed in around him. He had spent the last years of his
life seeking refuge in various countries, but was always forced
out as Rome advanced. He was sixty-two and, at his painless
death, had lived much longer than the tens of thousands of
men—Romans, Carthaginians, and mercenaries—whose lives
he was responsible for ending.

Around Hera's column at Capo Colonna burned the campfires of
Hannibal's Carthaginian army and, if ancient accounts are true,
of the mercenaries whose bodies would be left to rot along Kroton's beaches as the general sailed southwest to North Africa.
Livy—was he a Roman propagandist?—tells us that the mercenaries tried to take refuge in the "hitherto inviolate shrine" of
Hera's temple, but were "brutally butchered in [its] very
precincts." Some modern historians believe Hannibal slaughtered his army's horses—because there was no room for the animals in the boats that carried his troops to Carthage—not men.

Before he fled to North Africa, Hannibal reportedly set up a
large bronze plaque within the temple grounds, which Livy said
was "inscribed in Greek and Carthaginian to commemorate his
many military exploits." No one I talked to seems to know
where that bronze plaque rests today, if it ever existed at all.

I sit in the midst of the temple that now, except for the single column at my back, is stoneless, at least on the grass-covered surface, trying to visualize what it must have been like. All
I can conjure up is how Gissing, locked deep into delirium and
fever in his room at the Concordia, saw it in his imagination.
He wrote of these dreams:

"I saw the strand by [Kroton]; the promontory with its temple; not as I know the scene to-day, but as it must have looked

to those eyes more than two thousand years ago. The soldiers of Hannibal doing massacre, the perishing mercenaries, supported my closest gaze, and left no curiosity unsatisfied. . . . When I spoke of the experience to Dr. Sculco, he was much amused, and afterwards he often asked me whether I had had any more *visioni*. That gate of dreams was closed, but I shall always feel that, for an hour, it was granted me to see the vanished life . . . a world known to me only in ruined fragments."

I walked back to my car, drove past the German bunker and decided it was time to move on to lofty heights inland from the Ionian Sea. I would next go to Calabria's capital, Catanzaro, forty miles to Crotone's southwest, where the still feverish Gissing went, against his doctor's orders, to get out of the malarial and stagnant lower elevation, and to recover his health in fresh mountain air. Catanzaro was not a place for reflection about the Greeks; few, if any, likely stood on its high promontory. It was a place for recuperation.

Gissing certainly did not know then that the story of his visit to the mountaintop would give the world a southern Italian name that would live on: the last name of the proud owner of Hotel Centrale, Coriolano Paparazzo.

Chapter 17

Paparazzo's Kitchen

Catanzaro was Gissing's city of refuge and recuperation. Here he was bathed by the gentle breezes that swept away the cobwebs of illness he carried from the malarial plain of what was then called Cotrone. How things change in one hundred years!

Modern Crotone is now a healthy destination point. Its swamps were drained long ago and its water supply improved. Today, its beaches are regularly raked for the few tourists who venture this far south.

Catanzaro, meanwhile, still "the breezy height" Gissing described, is a much-changed, modern hilltop city with all the problems that designation implies. One of its great benefits is that it is the gateway to delightful villages higher up in the Calabrian Mountains.

I arrived, early afternoon, at Catanzaro Lido, the station that Gissing called the "marina," located along the Ionian Sea and several miles below the upper town. I did not know there was another train station, still higher up at the base of the promontory that holds this capital of Calabria, so I took a taxi and relied upon the driver for a hotel recommendation. It did not appear that Gissing's hotel, at least in its 1890s incarnation, still existed.

We wove our way up the serpentine road into Catanzaro and, once we reached the summit, a jammed, noisy, urban maze lay before us. It was mid-morning. Traffic was packed onto the narrow streets; the cab's meter ticked as we barely moved. It seemed that as many city buses as cars were stretched along the main roadway through the town, at least here defeating the theory that mass transit alone solves congestion. It still takes people to leave their cars at home!

Schoolchildren and pedestrians streamed at will through the traffic, moving from one side of the street to the other. It was gridlock, and the cab driver told me it was common. "Most of the day it is like this," he said.

Eventually, we made our way to a side street that swung around the brow of the hill. In between tall buildings that looked like they were built a century ago, I could look out and see where the Ionian Sea was supposed to be, my view stunned into submission by the coastal haze. We stopped at a small inn. I paid the driver and got a room for the night—a small, pathetic accommodation. I did not fight it since I figured I would be here only one night. I was in the third week of my journey and getting weary. Despite the poor quarters, the bed appeared comfortable and the room was warm.

Then, as is usual during undisciplined travel in Italy, when the traveler is willing to let things happen and not try to control events, I had a marvelous experience in an unexpected trip into the mountains.

It started after I left my squalid room, found an *osteria*, and ate a delicious meal. I climbed onto a city bus, just to let it carry me around Catanzaro so I could take in the sights. We wove through the outer perimeter, taking forever in the congestion. I could see that this mountaintop city had a more modern tinge to it than Gissing must have found.

There are certainly old buildings here, many containing upscale shops and what appeared to be much nicer hotels than the one my cab driver, in his hurry to get out of this city and back down to the coast, had deposited me in. But this town, I have read somewhere, has, over the centuries, been wracked by earthquakes and rebuilt several times. Gissing talked about one that hit the century before his visit—two centuries before mine—where not a house was left standing and people perished by the thousands.

So the buildings today bear scant resemblance to the town's medieval past. It was settled, probably during the ninth or tenth century C.E., long after the Greeks and the Romans, and during a time when the coastal inhabitants were driven inland to escape malaria and a constant stream of invaders from the sea. You see these towns everywhere on high promontories, established centuries ago for protection from both humans and microbes.

As the bus went around the outer curves, I could look down into the gorge below and the road that winds its way up the side. Even there, automobiles and trucks were packed end to end on both sides of the narrow roadway. People were walking up the hill to conduct their business in the town above. Once again I thought of the phrase "tyranny of traffic." Catanzaro, which started as a quiet mountain town, was, during this visit, a modern disaster of congestion and haze.

Eventually, the traffic thinned and the bus began following a ridge line that was turning from buildings into trees. The bus went up, up into the Calabrian mountains, and eventually I realized that it was not going to return to the city anytime soon. It had to at some point, I figured, so I merely sat back, enjoyed the view unfolding before me, and began to unwind from the traffic nightmare below. It was only the bus driver and me.

Ahead, a small church appeared at the bend in the road. The driver slowed and made a quick sign of the cross as he cranked the wheel to the left to make the turn. We passed along long ridges looking down into steep gorges with streams full of melted snow pouring off the high mountains above. It was paradise compared to where I had just come from. It was almost warm enough to open a window and enjoy the breeze.

About forty-five minutes into the trip, the bus pulled into a little village built up on the slopes. The driver told me he had a twenty-minute layover before resuming the journey back to Catanzaro. I got out and went into a small bar for a coffee. Its owner, a small, elderly Italian man, struck up a conversation as soon as he realized I was American. He spoke perfect English.

"I was in the U.S. Army," he told me. He had lived in Brooklyn, Texas, and Germany for many years, he said, but came back here, to his family's home province, to retire. "This is home," he said, waving his hand toward the still higher mountains that glistened through the windows of his bar.

I walked outside and sat on a bench overlooking a deep gorge, joining the bus driver, his gaze fixed in the distance as he smoked a cigarette. My Italian was not good enough to engage him in deep conversation, but I got the impression he cherished this part of his daily bus route: sitting in this little village with the name of Pentone, high on the Calabrian slopes and far, far away from the chaos of Catanzaro.

We returned, this time with one other passenger, a studious-looking young man who, along with the driver, made the sign of the cross as we passed the tiny church on the road below. I stepped off the bus in Catanzaro's main street, in the midst of hundreds of schoolchildren making their way home through bumper-to-bumper traffic, the cars honking and the children squealing with delight as they chased one another, dodging cars and giant orange buses.

Near one end of the town, I saw a small, freshly painted structure containing a new "car" for a funicular, one of those traction-driven contraptions one sees in some of the larger Italian cities, built along steep mountainsides. They hook onto steel rails and are propelled up and down the hills like the cable cars in San Francisco. Naples has at least three similar funicular systems plying the hills of that city's northwest crescent.

The sign on the door at the Catanzaro station said this funicular was closed. What a way to ease congestion. Commuters could park in the more open spaces below the town and ride the funicular up to work. Only in Italy, I thought, could something as helpful as this be shut down.

Several months later, in correspondence with an Italian friend who was born in Catanzaro, I learned the story. The local government when I was there had just finished restoring the funicular—hence the fresh paint and modern fixtures. The line had been closed for many years, in fact, several decades, because there was no money to run it. After restoration, officials still had to look for money to operate it.

I was told that nearly a year after my visit, the funicular is in full operation and doing much to ease the daily crush of traffic. The device is part of a grand tradition of mass transit in this town, my friend said, dating back to the early twentieth century. The older funicular took people up and down the hillside; at the top, a tram

Signor Paparazzo's Hotel Centrale in Catanzaro once occupied the building on the right, across the street from Gissing's "wonderful pharmacy," a place that still sports "a sort of griffin in wrought iron." The former Hotel Centrale is located at Corso Mazzini, n. 181. Filmmaker Federico Fellini used Paparazzo's name for a celebrity photographer in the 1960s movie *La dolce vita*—and the English language gained the term *"paparazzi."* In October 1999, Catanzaro officials installed a plaque commemorating Paparazzo, Gissing, Fellini and scriptwriter Ennio Flaiano.
Photo by Wulfhard Stahl

system on rails would take them from Piazza Roma to the very upper part of the city, an area known as Pontegrande. The tram tracks are long gone; the original tram station in Piazza Matteotti still stands, but it is now the site of a fast-food restaurant.

I spent the rest of the day walking through the town, but could not find any hotel named Centrale where Gissing spent his days of recuperation visiting with the British vice-consul, who turned out to be Italian instead of British—Don Pasquale. The

Scottish writer Douglas reports that a decade after Gissing was here, the vice-consul had died, and Douglas decided to skip going to this town since he could not visit with the man and talk about the Victorian writer, as Douglas had done with Dr. Sculco in Cotrone.

More than a year after my visit, I discovered through my Catanzaro friend, Vittorio, that the Centrale did exist well into the 1970s. "My parents tell me that they would go there for drinks and to eat," Vittorio told me. "I do not remember it as a hotel because I was a baby then."

He said the building, at Corso Mazzini, n. 181, is a beautiful structure, four floors above the ground and apparently built a short time before Gissing's visit in late 1897.

Meanwhile, Vittorio said that in the late 1990s, the building was vacant and for sale. For many years since the 1970s, it had housed the Medio Credito Centrale, an investment bank with, ironically, the word *Centrale* in its name.

I learned long after I left Catanzaro that city officials want to immortalize the building that held the old hotel. In late October 1999, a plaque was placed on its front. It would honor Gissing, Paparazzo, Fellini, and Fellini's Scripwriter Ennio Flaiano for their roles in plunging "paparazzi" into the modern lexicon, thereby bringing attention to the Calabrian capital.

But I knew none of this in early 1998. I returned to my squalid hotel and girded myself for spending a night in the tiny room, completely filled with a bed, a table, and a diminutive sink. The night clerk, a man in his early forties with one ear cocked toward the television room so he could overhear a soccer match, greeted me as I pushed my way inside through a narrow door, setting off a tinkling bell.

On impulse, I asked him if he knew the name Paparazzo.

"Yes, it is familiar," he replied. *"Perché?"* (Why?)

With my dictionary in hand and calling upon every ounce of my deficient knowledge of Italian, I told him about how the southern Italian name, written down in a famous travel narrative one hundred years earlier by a visitor to Catanzaro, came to symbolize the rise of celebrity during the last forty years of the twentieth century.

Coriolano Paparazzo was the owner of Gissing's hotel in Catanzaro, the Centrale. Signor Paparazzo was distressed that many of his guests ate in restaurants other than his own. He posted a note on the back of his guests' doors urging them to "bestow their kind favors on the restaurant of the house." By repeating this appeal, verbatim, in his book, Gissing granted Signor Paparazzo's name eternal life.

That happened because in 1958 the Italian film director Federico Fellini and his scriptwriter Ennio Flaiano were looking for a name to give their celebrity photographer in *La dolce vita*, the classic Italian film of Italy's postwar generation. By naming this aggressive photographer Paparazzo, Fellini and Flaiano gave the world the term *paparazzi*, the bane of every person trying to flee the burdens of celebrity.

I knew the sketchy details of the foundation of this word, and I knew that it had come from Gissing's *By the Ionian Sea*, which Flaiano said in an interview he had opened "at random," and the name caught his eye.

An article about this etymology appeared in *The Gissing Journal*. In it, the authors duly recorded that in 1982 there were seventeen Paparazzos in the Catanzaro telephone directory. I got the 1997 directory from the obliging night clerk and counted forty entries. "It is Sicilian in origin, I think," the desk clerk said.

Then his phone rang. It appeared to be his wife, or a close friend, calling. As I stood there, he recounted the whole story I had just relayed about Paparazzo, the Centrale, and Catanzaro. He did not know this before, he said into the receiver. *"Molto interessante."*

I walked up the three flights to my tiny room feeling comfort that somehow, in my fledgling use of the language, I had communicated an entire story to a sleepy desk clerk who said he found it "very interesting." He probably was just being kind, but I like to think he was just as fascinated by how that name from his small city became an icon for a generation.

The night was clear and, given the late hour, the traffic had disappeared. I knew it would begin again early in the morning and I was eager to head out of town. Gissing left, his health recovered, in a rented carriage. His destination was Squillace, the high mountain town farther to the south where a hero of Gissing's, Cassiodorus, who served one of the last Roman barbarian kings, may have been born. It also was near where Cassiodorus created his monastery for the religious life he sought after the fall of the Western Empire.

Gissing wanted to spend a night there. He arrived in a raging storm and had, within the space of a few hours, the worst experience of his trip, aside from his illness; and he fled Squillace in disgust.

Chapter 18

Bridge with No Road

I awoke in my room high on the third floor of the little inn in Catanzaro wishing I had a Signor Paparazzo to talk with over breakfast. I could hear the traffic beginning, far below, even though the hour was early. Light, just breaking from the direction of the Ionian Sea miles away, was beginning to stroke the sides of the ravines that sweep past, far below, this fragile, earthquake-prone city. I would leave this morning, after my breakfast of *cornetto con crema* and double espresso.

After all these years of visiting Italy and frequenting the growing number of places in my hometown that now sell espresso, I need more than the single shot in the morning. I need to sip something while I munch on my breakfast roll and read whatever English-language newspaper I can find. A double barely satisfies me. I could have what Italians call an *Americano*, which consists of the same amount of steam-driven coffee as a single shot of espresso, but heavily diluted with hot water so that it fills an American-size coffee cup. That, to me, is inadequate. Better to pay for a double, or even a triple, espresso, to start the day off properly!

My bare-bones hotel did not offer such a *prima colazione* (breakfast), so I left my bag behind the desk and stepped out into the traffic for a dodge-and-weave across the street to a coffee bar near the corner. While there, I purchased a bus ticket to get me down the hill to the train station below the town. From that point, I would head toward Squillace, which was Gissing's goal once he left the hospitality of Signor Paparazzo and the British vice-consul, Don Pasquale.

Gissing was reinvigorated from his few days in Catanzaro and finally well enough to resume his journey through the South. He was en route to the final city on his Magna Graecia itinerary, Reggio di Calabria. But he hoped to stop for the night at Squillace, known to the Greeks as Skylletion and to the Romans as Scylacium. Of greater interest to Gissing was that Scylacium was reputed to be the ancestral home of Cassiodorus, a descendant of Bruttian natives who were in this land long before the Greeks arrived more than one thousand years earlier.

Cassiodorus, in the early to mid-sixth century C.E., served the barbarian Roman kings near the end of the once mighty Western Empire. He served as prefect of Italy and as a royal administrator and draftsman.

The day I chose for my journey was bright and crisp. In reality, the journey by train to Squillace's coastal station is less than an hour from Catanzaro. Gissing had opted for a carriage because he thought it would be quicker, since he would need a carriage anyway to get from the station up to the town in the hills beyond. He ran into a tempest that filled the steep gorges on the approach to Squillace with roaring water, the waters' roar competing with the wind to drown all civilized sound from the Englishman's ears. From the station during my journey, I, too, would need a carriage, in the form of an automobile, to go up into the town.

The ride down from the upper Catanzaro station to Catanzaro Lido, the small tourist area along the Ionian Sea where I would change for Squillace, follows the same route as the train Gissing rode up to the lofty city. He described being surrounded by fields and orange groves. "All around lay orchards of orange trees, the finest I had ever seen, and over their solid masses of dark foliage, thick-hung with ripening fruit, poured the splendour of the western sky. Beyond, the magic sea, purple and crimson as the sun descended upon the vanishing horizon. Eastward, above the slopes of Sila, stood a moon almost at its full, the yellow of an autumn leaf, on a sky soft-flushed with rose."

My description is not as enchanting. When I rolled down from the upper station to the Lido station, I, too, passed through orange groves and fields, but I am sure they are not as expansive today as they were ten decades ago. Along the short twenty-minute route are homes and businesses, and around the station a large, plain commercial area has filled in Gissing's wondrous spaces.

Still, the morning was a delight, and I headed toward Squillace with as much enthusiasm as did Gissing. But I knew how his story turned out. I had no idea what my story would be.

Until I read Gissing's narrative, I had never heard of Cassiodorus. This historic figure charmed the British writer for reasons I can only guess at. Perhaps it was because Cassiodorus continued to live a full and productive life when he left the employ of the fading barbarian rulers in Rome, serving as scribe and writing diplomatic letters for the most famous of them, Theodoric.

A Christian, Cassiodorus made a failed attempt with Pope Agapetus to create a school of Christian higher education in Rome. He retired in C.E. 538 during the Gothic wars, went to Constantinople and served in the Eastern Empire for a few years, eventually making it back to his home in the area around Roman Scylacium, now known as Squillace.

There he created a monastery somewhere near the town alongside his family estate and made perhaps his greatest contribution to the Western world. The historian J. B. Bury, in his *History of the Later Roman Empire*, called what Cassiodorus did in ancient times "a novelty." The old monk created a *scriptorium*, or writing room, in the monastery and had his monks copy "both pagan and Christian books, working at night by the light of self-filling 'mechanical lamps.' It is well known that the preservation of our heritage of Latin literature is mainly due to monastic copyists. The originator of the idea was Cassiodorus."

Perhaps Gissing's attraction to this prolific old man was his full life and singular accomplishments. Cassiodorus wrote histories of the Goths, and of Rome and the Roman world. He preserved Western literature. Such a life would impress Gissing, as it should all of us. His death is believed to be in 585 C.E. If that date is correct, Cassiodorus would have been ninety-five years old.

I left the main north–south highway near the Squillace station and followed a narrow, two-lane blacktop that, given its placement along the fields and hills leading to the tiny white town perched on the high ridge ahead, had to follow Gissing's path to the town through the storm. The road pitched and rolled over the fields, gradually gaining height, and then swept up a mountainside in steep curves. I exulted that the road ahead appeared to move around to the town's backside rather than go straight up the steep side facing the sea. This was precisely as Gissing had described it. And here I began to contemplate what I would find.

Gissing had a horrible time in what he described as a tumble-down village—an experience I suspect would be similar to a traveler from a cosmopolitan United States city, say New York, going into a primitive-looking, newly formed, wild West town, during a massive thunderstorm, in the mid 1800s. Gissing found mud and water flowing down steep streets and, faint with hunger, he stepped out of his carriage, ankle deep in water and in front of what appeared to be the town's Osteria Centrale and Albergo Nazionale.

The structures and surrounding buildings, to Gissing's eye, personified squalor of the worst kind. They made his room at the Concordia—and my room at the inn in Catanzaro—look like palaces.

As he wandered the streets that "in the ordinary sense of the word, do not exist," following his absolutely unsatisfactory meal laced with what he was sure was poisonous wine, he looked into the houses of the people and saw unparalleled squalor. Gissing thought of the phrase he had once heard spoken in a small town between Rome and Naples: *C'è miseria* (There is nothing but poverty).

Squillace has changed. I drove up the mountain's backside and into a tan and light yellow paradise. Streets, albeit as steep as a century earlier, do exist. It was about noon, and people stood outside their doors talking to one another.

An elderly woman, in a bright coat of many colors—an

unusual sight in the South, where elderly women, usually all widows, wear black—was trudging up one of the narrow streets, paved and with steps cut into the middle. She leaned forward with every step, solidly planting her walking stick as far uphill as she could reach. Then she would walk two or three small steps up to it, holding on as if she were moving headlong into a ferocious gale.

White, gentle clouds were moving over the summit and the morning's promise of sun was fading; there was no wind, just the steepness of grade that I assumed she had been trudging most of her long life.

I parked and started to walk up into the town, looking to see if I could find any evidence of Osteria Centrale or Albergo Nazionale. Of course I could not. Those businesses were long gone, as were their "ill-looking" proprietors. Again, as I did everywhere but Crotone, I could only look and wonder where the buildings were that Gissing described so vividly. In Squillace, the buildings easily dated back to a time much earlier than his visit. The buildings had to be here, and possibly the owners' descendants.

I moved higher up into the town, toward the Norman castle that Gissing saw on its perch at the town's highest point. It was fenced off and its gate locked. I had wanted to climb its rampart and view the valley below. I turned and walked toward a small group of people. The oldest of the group, a middle-aged man, was pointing out the homes and sights. "Did you see the castle?" he asked me in Italian. "*Sì,*" I said. "*Ma è chiuso*" (But it is closed).

I turned to make my way back down to my car. The man, Giuseppe Cerullo, grabbed my arm and asked me to stay. "Go with us," he said, explaining that the three young people with him were students and he was giving them a tour of his historic village. My Italian was not up to full comprehension, but I gleaned enough to make the unexpected diversion worthwhile.

We passed a nondescript house, and Giuseppe pointed to its Arabic-style window. This was a house built by Saracens in the Middle Ages, he said. The house had been stuccoed and painted dozens of times in the centuries since, but the distinctive window and its North African design endured. He pointed to a giant boulder under the corner of another house. The Saracens built their homes on such rocks, he said, that are embedded deep into the earth, on "natural" foundations.

We walked past another home, with a round circle of earth in the midst of the pavement in front, about four or five feet in diameter. Here, Giuseppe said, stood a giant palm tree, "for many, many, many decades, perhaps a century."

Finally, he took us to a tiny abandoned structure jammed between restored Saracen-era homes. This, he said, was a Christian church, dating back to the Middle Ages. "It has been deconsecrated," he said, meaning it is no longer an active church. The building was locked, but Giuseppe knocked on the door of a nearby house. A man, who had seen us out the window, opened his door and walked out, holding a large, rusty key. The man unlocked the empty church's door, using both hands to turn the key, then swinging the door open as wide as his proud smile. *"Molto vecchio"* (Very old), he said to us as we walked into the dim interior lit only by sunlight edging its way in through narrow, vertical windows.

All ornamentation, of course, had been removed, including the tiles from the floor. In one spot, just in front of where the tiny altar would have sat, was a disturbed area that looked like the rectangular shape of a grave. *"Forse una tomba"* (Perhaps a tomb), Giuseppe said. I did not have the language ability to ask if the excavation was being done by archaeologists or by the owners. Perhaps I did not want to know.

Near the tiny town's main square, I said good-bye to Giuseppe and his three young friends. I asked him if I could reimburse him for his services. No, no, he said quickly. "It is my pleasure to show you my village."

Such is the passion I find in Italy. Particularly, I find it in little towns far off the tourist track. Squillace is not a tourist town; Crotone seems to cater only to locals and some Italian tourists; Taranto is little known to the outside world except to German travelers, my cab-driver friend had told me days earlier.

In each city—even in clogged and smoky Catanzaro where a night clerk politely listened to my story about Signor Paparazzo and made me feel as though I had just enriched his life by telling the tale—I found unexpected adventure and people whose pride in their home cities flows through every pore. It is what keeps me coming back.

I still had one more stop to make before I reached Squillace's train *stazione* miles away along the coast. Before I had left Giuseppe and his group of students, we had stood along the ramparts of the closed and austere Norman castle that dominated the town, looking across the small, narrow valley below. There, just off the road that would take me from the town, standing across a tiny stream and next to an olive grove filled with ancient trees, lay an arched bridge, with grass growing on the top.

There was no road going to either side of the bridge. Giuseppe had seen that I saw it. "It was built in the twelfth century," he had said. That means it could have been a Norman

This twelfth century C.E. bridge, likely built by the Normans, sits in a farmer's field below the town of Squillace. High on the hill is a Norman castle. Much of the town's architecture was influenced by the Normans and their predecessors, the Saracens. Gissing only spent a few unhappy hours in this small Calabrian village. He was drawn here because it was the home of his beloved Cassiodorus, the monk who served one of the last Roman Gothic kings during the fall of the western Empire, and who initiated the monastic tradition of copying ancient texts, thereby preserving them for later generations. *Photo by John Keahey*

bridge. An old road, now buried beneath a farmer's fields, must have once gone over the top of it. *"Interessante, eh?"* Giuseppe said to me, with a wink.

Now I drove out of the town, rounding the first curve of the road that would take me toward the sea. Just above the olive grove, I parked the car and stood, looking down at the bridge. It definitely appeared to be on private property. I hesitated, but the urge was too great. I walked down, along the side of the grove, through a field that had lain fallow through the winter. I reached the stream, crossed the corner of the grove, and climbed on top of a low concrete wall that skirted the front of the arched, stone bridge.

I knelt down and looked at it closely. Knowing nothing about architecture, I could only surmise that the Normans, or perhaps Saracens who had earlier created much of Squillace, had built it. I knew from history books that the Normans had pushed westward from Italy's heel and conquered much of Calabria by the eleventh century C.E. Here it was, on a farmer's property. Untouched and intact after centuries. What a thing for a child to play on! I thought. Surely the owners knew what they had here.

After a few moments, I turned and began the quarter-mile trudge back up along the fallow field. Then I heard one low bark, looked up, and saw the farmer's dog straining at a taut chain, trying to come toward me. There was no growling, no frenzied barking, just one low warning bark. This was not a dog to mess with. Carrying my innate fear up the hill with me, the same fear that earlier had visited me in Táranto, I made it back to the car in record time. I did not want to find out if that dog could break its sturdy chain.

With my pulse rate slowly returning to normal, I began to think about Reggio, for centuries an outpost on Italy's bumpy toe. It was Gissing's, and my, last stop before each of us, a century apart, would return to Rome.

Chapter 19

In the Lair of Cassiodorus

I reached Squillace *stazione*, along the coast and miles below the old town, and found it bathed in sunlight. The Ionian Sea beyond was placid, and turning before my eyes from gray to blue. A passing storm, which had scattered rain throughout the morning, had moved far out to sea. Far away, I could see dark gray clouds in the sky that touched the water. But here the sun was warm, and the train for Reggio di Calabria, mine and Gissing's last stop in our Ionian odyssey, was waiting.

I have a regret here. I walked into the station and saw the southbound train sitting there. I had only a few minutes before it left and, too hurriedly, decided that rather than wait an hour or two for the next one as Gissing had done, I would climb on and settle in, expecting to arrive at Reggio in the late afternoon.

As the train moved slowly out of the station and south toward Reggio along the coastline, which makes up the front half of the bottom of Italy's foot, I reread Gissing's description of his two-hour layover at this very station. He had had an adventure here, one that I could try to re-create. Quickly, I thought about getting off at the next station, heading back to Squillace station, and taking the walk he did.

Alas, I succumbed to the rigors of being on the road and alone for three weeks, sat back in my comfortable seat, and watched the rain squall far out in the Ionian.

From the *stazione*, Gissing had filled his two hours by walking along the tracks "towards the black furrowed mountain side." There is a tunnel here, now as then, that allows the train to shoot through the final ridge of the Apennine range—a point that Gissing called the promontory of the Mons Moscius. I never saw that name on any of my maps, but it is the spot, according to Gissing and my Italian Touring Club map, where the Apennines, which run nearly the length of Italy from high up in the boot, disappear into the sea. Both he and I had criss-crossed these mountains for weeks and, each in our own time, now were at the end of this historic mountain range and our respective journeys.

In these mountains, and in the hills beyond this ridge well into Italy's toe where the high mass of the Aspromonte dominates, early Greeks pushed upward from the coast during the fifth century B.C.E. and onto high promontories and mountain-tops all along this bottom of Italy. They were driven there by the fierce Italic tribes, and mosquitoes, and isolated for centuries. This isolation preserved their Greek language, and, I am told, an archaic form of Greek is still spoken in places here by the people known as Grecanici.

But like those remaining in the coastal cities, this barrier of language did not protect them from the successive sweeps of invaders. Despite these influences, these ancient Greeks continued to practice their Greek Orthodox faith, I have read, resisting Catholicism well into the fourteenth century C.E.

But Gissing's thoughts during his two-hour layover did not turn to the Greeks. He was still thinking about the time of Cassiodorus and early Christianity's ascendancy in the city of Rome, with popes replacing emperors and kings as the western Roman Empire crumbled. Near here, Gissing believed, was the monastery of Cassiodorus, where the monks piously copied their Latin manuscripts. The railroad tracks he walked along—the very path my train was taking—crossed the Fiume di Squillace, the river known in Cassiodorus's time as the Pellena, which flowed, full of fish, along the monastery's grounds.

In fact, his monastic compound has been called the Vivarium, a word that today refers to a container or place that contains small animals. In his day, it referred to the fish ponds he reputedly built along the river—a place where fish could be kept in a natural habitat.

"Here, then, I stood in full view of the spot which I had so often visioned in my mind's eye. Much of the land hereabout—probably an immense tract of hill and valley—was the old monk's patrimonial estate," Gissing wrote. Because of my foolish, impulsive decision, I had to content myself with flashing by on the coastal train rather than ambling along the tracks toward the tunnel through the Mons Moscius as Gissing had done. I saw the tunnel coming up and quickly glanced through my compartment window down toward the water.

It was along the tracks, here at this point, where Gissing met a group of railway workers who climbed with him down the rocky shoreline to the sea. These men, though illiterate, all knew of Cassiodorus and showed Gissing a small cave along the shore that Gissing speculated once must have connected with the Squillace, then Pellena, River. Over the centuries, he surmised, the river, like the Coscile and the Crati Rivers to the north at Sybaris/Thurii/Copia, had changed course, wandering away from the cave and far away from where it was nearly fifteen hundred years earlier along the ancestral lands of Cassiodorus.

Gissing tried to pay the men for their help and information. "They refused with entire dignity—grave, courteous, firm. . . . With handshaking, we took kindly leave of each other. Such self-respect is the rarest thing in Italy south of Rome, but in Calabria I found it more than once."

I thought, once again, about the many times I, too, had found such graciousness and self-respect. I remember the guide in Squillace just a few miles away from this spot. He, like the railroad workers one hundred years earlier, had smilingly and kindly rebuffed my offer of grateful remuneration. He had shaken my hand warmly, telling me how it pleased him that someone cared about this town. I remember the man who came out of his house with the huge iron key to let us into the abandoned church, happy to divert his attention, for no monetary reward, for a group of strangers. I remember my guide at Sybaris/Thurii/Copia who spent a morning trudging with me through the water-soaked ruins, explaining with enthusiasm how the ancient cities were unfolding before her and her colleagues' eyes. I remember the fisherman along Taranto's Little Sea who calmed his pack of guard dogs and talked to me for half an hour about catching crabs and shrimp, the cab driver who pointed out my dropped one-hundred-thousand-lira note, the young Pugliese bus driver telling me about wild dogs and life in the South.

I reflected on all this, alone again in my train compartment, as I zipped through the tunnel that took me out of the Apennines and along the coast of the Aspromonte, the last great spur of mountain massif that rises, in a series of terraces, above the Ionian Sea. For someone who spoke little Italian and had spent three weeks talking with people who spoke little English, I had learned a great deal about graciousness and pride.

What I did not notice—and apparently Gissing did not notice it either—was that just on the other side of that tunnel, at the end of a short road that drops off to the left, is the purported tomb of Cassiodorus. At least that is what the inscription says, a friend told me long after I returned home.

Knowing how myth often becomes "reality," I do not know if the bones of Cassiodorus truly are there. It does make for an appealing tourist attraction.

I recall visiting the spot in Idaho where a marker designates the final resting place of my mother's ashes, and discovering—after dozens of visits, complete with flowers and tearful remembrances—that her ashes had never actually been placed there. They were several hundred feet away, in a tiny storage room, locked behind the cemetery offices.

I wasn't present when, much later, the cemetery custodian over the telephone promised me that he placed them beneath the marker. Short of reopening the small box beneath the plaque, I have to take his word for it, just like modern visitors to European shrines have to take it on faith that Napoleon's bones, say, really are in that tomb in Paris, or that Cassiodorus's remains really are under that stone slab near the train tunnel in Calabria.

Chapter 20

The End of the Toe

It was late in the day when the train pulled into Reggio. I walked outside of the station and into the warm, tree-lined square full of city buses waiting to begin their routes. I had a map, and it appeared that I wanted to move north several blocks toward the city center, about a mile away. The first bus driver I talked to told me where to catch a bus for the center, and said I could find a hotel there. Within minutes, I was lodged in a moderately priced room, complete with television and all the amenities. By this time, I was desperate for an English-speaking news station. But only Italian-language stations were represented. I went out and wandered the streets, joining the crowds of pedestrians along the traffic-free Corso Garibaldi.

What a delight Reggio is, with its orderly streets and strict limitations on automobiles. The Corso, except for certain times of day, is off limits to cars. Only buses and people can use the wide boulevard during the afternoon and evening hours.

I did see one horrifying scene here: A young miniskirted

The cathedral in Reggio di Calabria, Gissing's last stop on his tour of Magna Graecia, is newly restored. The city was heavily damaged by a major earthquake a few years after his visit and was bombed during World War II. Little of what Gissing saw here remains. *Photo by John Keahey*

mother, a cigarette dangling from the side of her mouth, sitting on a tiny scooter, her tiny daughter standing between the knees of the mother, who was weaving in and out among the pedestrians and buses.

Ah, Italy. The land where seat belts are sat on and a toddler stands on a scooter's floorboard, holding on for dear life and shrieking with joy at the wind in her hair!

Not much of the city Gissing saw remains. He was there during December 1897. It was razed by an earthquake in 1908, and rebuilt with wider streets and low, reinforced-concrete buildings. Centuries earlier, unlike most conquerors, the Romans treated the city well; after all, Rhegion, so named by the Greeks and later named Rhegium by the Romans, had remained loyal to Rome during the Punic Wars, including Hannibal's invasion.

Along the Lungomare Matteotti, the street along the harbor just down from the Corso Garibaldi, are only a dribbling of Greek ruins—a short wall. Just a few hundred feet away are the remains of a Roman bath. Not much else of the ancient city exists. But standing here with my back to the city, after dropping down from the traffic-free Corso during my early evening walk, I could gaze across, as Gissing did, to the east coast of Sicily, just a few miles away.

To the northwest blinked the lights of Messina; to the southwest, shrouded in haze and out of sight, would be the slopes of Etna, a volcano, like Vesuvius, that still threatens all life on its fertile Sicilian slopes.

Reggio has a poor harbor, but it must have been chosen by the ancients for its commanding position along the Strait of Messina. It was an ideal trading spot, bringing together ships from the Greek world south of Italy, the colonists in Sicily just a few hundred yards across the strait, and those plying the waters along Italy's west coast. The original Greek settlers here were always under threat of invasion, first by fellow Greek colonists from other cities, later by the other nationalities that foraged along this impressive coastline.

Eventually, the Siracusans from the southeast coast of Sicily needed Rhegion as a bridgehead for the defense of their island. After a long siege that ended in 386 B.C.E., the Greeks from Syrakusai, modern Siracusa, dismantled the wall I saw the remains of, and built a palace along the waterfront. Eventually, after the Romans took over following Hannibal's departure from Kroton farther north, new colonists were sent by the Roman emperor Augustus just before the birth of Christ to newly renamed Rhegium, which flourished throughout the imperial Roman period.

My first morning here was spent in the Museo Nazionale della Magna Graecia. Gissing toured these displays. He had flipped back through the pages of the museum's guest book and discovered the name, on its first page, of "François Lenormant, Membre de l'Institut de France," the date 1882. There was no such book for me to flip back through, to see if I could discover Gissing's name, or to record my own. I later found out that the old one is filed away. But it was hard to determine whether the building he visited was the same one I saw. So much has changed here in the last one hundred years, particularly after the giant earthquake eleven years following his visit.

Gissing talked about seeing a plaque on a sidewalk honoring a war hero, a common soldier. It would be impossible to find it, even if it still existed. Gissing scholars, who delve into such minutiae, have found a street in Reggio named for the soldier—perhaps they got the name "Emilio Cuzzocrea" from Gissing's diary—although it would appear that the plaque Gissing saw no longer exists.

But the museum I visited is one of the best in Italy. It, joined with the new ones at Sibari and Metaponto, and the venerable one in Taranto, provides a great repository for the wonders of Magna Graecia. In linear fashion, the Reggio museum covers Bronze Age and Iron Age Calabria, the archaic and Hellenic Greek civilizations, and the Roman period. I had seen a great deal of these types of antiquities elsewhere and moved quickly through the displays.

A Sweet and Glorious Land

One of two Riace Bronzes, pulled out of the sea in the 1970s from the shallow harbor of Calabria's Riace Marina on the underside of Italy's toe, is housed in Reggio's archaeological museum. The two bronzes were restored here and have their own earthquake-proof display area in the vast museum.

Photo by John Keahey

Here, I was more eager to see the Riace Bronzes, those incredible life-size statues pulled out of twenty-five feet of seawater nearly one thousand yards off the coast at nearby Riace Harbor in 1972. Riace is where modern-day immigrants, Kurds and North Africans, poured into Italy every year during the late 1990s, but it also is where a Greek ship, carrying goods to and from Greece, must have wrecked thousands of years ago.

These bronzes were painstakingly restored over a five-year period in this museum, and toured the world before being lodged permanently in the amphitheater where the restoration took place. Now they stand, in their own large, bright, humidity-controlled room, with their own guard, who obligingly let me take photographs, as long as I did not use my flash. *"Senza flash!"* he told me politely, wagging his index finger.

The statues are not behind protective glass but out in the open, positioned on a special platform-fixture system designed to keep them upright during an earthquake—a frequent event in this southern Calabrian city. Once again, as in Táranto and Síbari, I had the museum, and this room, to myself. Just me, the guard, and the bronze representation of two fierce, golden Greek warriors or athletes. They have similar outlines and their measurements are nearly the same, but each stance is different, and the heads are held at different angles. Scientists speculate they may have been part of a cluster of heroic statues; they may have been done by different artists and at different dates.

The restored statues, even after centuries in the sea, have vivid features. The pupils of their eyes are inlaid with ivory and limestone, the corneas are glassy, their lips, nipples, and eyelashes are copper, their teeth silver. With smooth "skin" and bulging veins, they appear as if Michelangelo, the Renaissance sculptor of the sixteenth century C.E., who more than one thousand years later gave birth out of marble to the magnificent *David*, had a hand in their creation.

These bronzes are a fine example of how advanced the 500 B.C.E. Greek sculptors really were, the ancient anonymous equivalents of Michelangelo. It took centuries after this glorious period for artisans to recapture the techniques that had been used to create the Riace Bronzes.

My trip through a small part of Magna Graecia, like Gissing's one hundred years before, was ending.

On my last morning, before catching the train to Sicily

where I would spend a few days and then head for Rome and an airplane home, the desk clerk at my hotel offered to take me to the roof. There, he said, I would get a clear, unobstructed view of the city to the east and of Sicily across the Strait of Messina to the west. He quietly, and patiently, waited at the doorway while I paced along the roof's edge.

The city rises up in concentric circles, ringing the tip of the Aspromonte that makes up the toe of Italy. The *centro* is strung out, like pearls on a necklace around the base of this giant massif. Reggio is quiet, pleasant.

I find it hard to believe that in recent years the *'ndrangheta*, or Calabrian Mafia, has had so much power in the city's construction rackets and is deeply involved in fierce extortion scams, and in international drug dealing and arms trafficking.

I have read about the years of misguided central-government policies, as I have seen elsewhere throughout the South, that have led to huge unemployment levels—roughly fifty percent in Reggio alone for those under age twenty-five. I did not see them, but I understand there are open sewers in some of this quiet city's poorer neighborhoods, and that tap water here is undrinkable.

The day before, I had looked for a wonderful old building that Gissing had described, the slaughterhouse he said was south of the train station, but I could not find it. Perhaps today's train station is in a different location. Perhaps the slaughterhouse was destroyed in the 1908 earthquake or during World War II bombing runs.

Many of the owners of the shops I entered during my walks pay tribute, protection money, to the crime syndicate. In the mid-1990s, an energetic prosecutor found a decapitated cat impaled on the gate of his country house. A journalist with *La*

Gazzetta del Sud has been the owner of three cars destroyed in separate car bombings. According to an in-depth article published in Britain's *Independent* in 1996, the crime families have more licensing power for small businesses than the city government. All of the shops in the city's market in Piazza del Popolo, the article said, are illegal, "licensed" by the *'ndrangheta*. Thankfully, most of this is missed by the casual tourist here for the warmth, the culture, the sense of history, and the spectacular views.

Instead we see typical Italian "street theater." I am reminded of this by Luigi Barzini's *The Italians*, his 1964 classic that beautifully describes the nature of the Italian people—characterizations that got him into trouble, I understand, with his fellow countrymen. Barzini talks about how Italians "perform" when talking to one another, how they raise their voices, gesture with hands, arms, the entire body.

Over the years, I have seen this again and again. I would think I was watching two Italians in heated, perhaps even deadly, exchange, their voices rising, one on top of the other, on street corners or on crowded trains. Then, suddenly, at what seemed to be the height of the debate, they would stop, smile, and shake hands or embrace, wishing each other well as they parted company.

In Reggio late one afternoon, I saw such theater played out in the street, in the aftermath of a three-car collision during rush hour. A car in the rear banged into the car in front, pushing it into a third car. Three drivers, all muscular, well dressed, and male, simultaneously jumped out of their vehicles, shouting, waving, and pointing fingers of blame. The heated debate rose in pitch over perhaps five minutes. Then, when the driver in the rear acknowledged he actually may have caused the problem, the mood of the two in front, their mastery of their automobiles unassailed, instantly turned calm and cordial. The three men quickly exchanged names and addresses and, presumably, insurance numbers. They patted each other on the shoulder and shook hands, warmly shouting *"Ciao! Ciao!"* as if they were saying farewell to long-lost friends. Each climbed into his slightly damaged car and sped off in a separate direction.

From my rooftop, I turned to the Strait of Messina and watched a line of ships, slowly following astern of one another, crossing south to north through the strait, so rich in mythology and real history. Through here, across my very line of sight, the Mediterranean world sailed, as each empire grew out of the dust, developed into great and powerful, but brutal, conquerors, and, in turn, each disappeared back into dust.

Today along this slight cusp of asphalt-covered land, only fragments of their towers, walls, temples, and forums remain visible. Through it all, the Greeks developed their art and their culture, and that is what the Romans, in turn, with their own embellishments, passed down to the rest of the Western world.

I thought again of Herodotus, that amazing Greek historian who was the first to write, in prose, of the follies of men, taking them out of the veil of mythology and making them human. Peter Romm, in his study of the historian, quotes from the ancient writer who "quotes" Solon, a historic figure, discoursing on the inevitable sorrow of human life and why wealth—and power—cannot make up for those sorrows:

"One must look to the end of every matter, how it will turn out; for the god has shown a glimpse of happiness to many men, then destroyed them root and branch."

So it was with the ancient civilizations and their peoples. Each had a "glimpse of happiness," a moment of glory and power, and each has disappeared. Egypt lasted several thousand years as the world's greatest power, replaced by Greece for several hundred years after the Greeks descended from earlier civilizations farther east, beyond the Aegean; Rome lasted a thousand years, grinding into dust its greatest challengers, the Carthaginians, before weakened, decadent Rome itself was devastated by the barbarians in the West and the Saracens in the East. Almost all have become forgotten races that ended up absorbed by other peoples.

In modern times, the Germans launched a thousand-year Reich, only to see it dissolve after a brief, brutal decade. Americans, conquerors in the nineteenth century and liberators in the twentieth, have lasted as a united people barely more than two hundred years. We still forget what "old" is. Where will our civilization be in one thousand years? What part of the earth, what nation, what people, still to be formed into new governments, will dominate then? Are we living our "glimpse of happiness" now, just to have it snatched away in the centuries ahead?

Within a few days, I would return to Rome and head home—on April 13, 1998. George Gissing, I knew, left Rome one hundred years and a day before me—on April 12, 1898—heading north on the 2:30 train where, according to his diary, he spent a sleepless night. He arrived in Berlin on April 14, stopping briefly to visit a friend before returning to England. He, too, following his Ionian adventure, had spent time—several weeks, contrasted with my few days—in Rome sight-seeing and visiting with his friends Arthur Conan Doyle and H. G. Wells, and the impressionable and enchanting Brian Ború Dunne.

But first I wanted to spend a few days in Sicily, where Gissing longed to go but never made it.

I walked through the door held open by the gracious and

kindly desk clerk, picked up my luggage, and walked several blocks toward the port of Reggio di Calabria. There I caught the small state railroad–operated boat that would carry me across the strait to the Sicilian port of Messina.

Acknowledgments

For help in this task, I have many people to thank. I begin with my daughter, Jennifer, and sons, Todd and Brad, whose excitement over the project reinvigorated me on a regular basis. I also am grateful to Giovanni Maschero, the Italian vice-consul in Salt Lake City, Utah, who contacted key people for me to speak with in Rome; and to Vittorio Cammarota, a native of Catanzaro in Calabria, who works for the Italian Cultural Institute in Washington, D.C. Vittorio answered many questions about his region, tracked down key photographs, and queried his parents, Giuseppina and Beda Cammarota, about Signor Paparazzo's Hotel Centrale in Catanzaro. His sister, Maria Cammarota, provided a photo of the hotel.

I owe several debts to a cadre of devoted Gissing scholars. His first major biographer, Professor Jacob (Jack) Korg of the University of Washington in Seattle, and I developed a lively correspondence in which we reviewed aspects of Gissing's life that have come to light over the three and a half decades since the professor's biography was first published.

I also developed a delightful letter and fax exchange with

Acknowledgments

Pierre Coustillas of the University of Lille in France, who is working on a comprehensive Gissing biography. Coustillas also was scheduled to publish, in late 1999 in *The Gissing Journal*, an article about his 1998 visit to Gissing sites in Calabria. Pierre and I discovered that his October 1998 trip followed nearly the same path of my early 1998 and early 1999 trips. We conducted them each unbeknownst to the other. He spent a day with me in July 1999 at his home in northern France, showing me his private Gissing "museum" and his twelve hundred fifty–volume collection of Gissing works in a variety of editions and languages. This collection includes a small portion of Gissing's personal library, and a bookcase and chair owned by Gissing in the later years of his life.

I also thank his friend and colleague Paul F. Mattheisen of Binghamton University, New York, who helped me with Gissing photographs and offered much moral support through a remarkable series of letters to me. Peter Morton of Flinders University of South Australia helped with critical dates.

My gratitude extends to Salt Lake City rare-book dealer and friend Kent Walgren, who never failed to find any obscure, out-of-print book I needed for this research, and who encouraged me—visit after visit to his small, comfortable shop—to keep writing. And I often relied on the advice of fellow Italophile Mike Homer of Salt Lake City, who tipped me off about Gissing's relationship with Arthur Conan Doyle and H. G. Wells, and who caught errors in my brief recounting of Italy's unification. Others who provided encouragement and support are Gary Bergera, Ron Priddis, Bill Slaughter, and Jim Ure, all of Salt Lake City.

I have particularly deep gratitude for Professor Baldassare Conticello, an eminent Italian archaeologist and specialist in the Greek colonization of southern Italy. He spent several hours over two days with me in Rome, educating a not-too-knowledgeable journalist with a twenty-five-year-old bachelor's degree in U.S. history about the nuances of ancient history.

And there is my friend and colleague Paul Paolicelli, whom I first met in Rome in 1992. His love and excitement for Italy have never failed to motivate me, and it was he who at first gently, then more forcibly, pushed me to get this book written and published, and who led me by the hand to my agent, Tony Seidl.

Another Roman friend comes to mind: Maria Findlow, who walked around Naples with me one cold, windy, wet March morning, showing me the places she loves. She made a special trip to that city months later to gather key information I had missed.

I cannot forget Isora Migliari, a researcher at the Sybaris/Thurii/Copia excavation who rescued me when the site was closed and offered a private tour. She shed more light in a few short hours on what was happening there than I had found in all my reading.

I have people closer to home to thank, too: Mark Trahant, one of my former editors in the daily newspaper business, now a columnist in Seattle, who read the manuscript to make sure that the narrative flowed and to ensure that I never mixed metaphors; and my dear Italian-language teacher, Marné Milner, now of Rebersburg, Pennsylvania, who corrected my sometimes shaky use of Italian.

I also must thank another former newspaper editor, David Ledford, now running his own daily in Sioux Falls, South Dakota. He taught me more about writing and storytelling in the three years I directly worked for him than I had learned in some thirty years of practicing various forms of journalism. His influence is on every page.

Finally, I thank Connie Disney, my friend and companion, who has tolerated my incurable love for Italy and my need to return there, year after year. She tolerates my growing piles of books about Italy, its history, its archaeology, and its culture, always allowing room for them amidst her own considerable collection. She encouraged me to do this book from the first moment the idea hit and never backed off from that encouragement, pushing me to make an additional trip when I realized I had more to do and see. She has been my first, best reader, marking in red ink confusing passages and demanding that I do better. Without her, this book could not have been written.

—John Keahey
Salt Lake City, Utah
November 1999

Select Bibliography

Adkins, Lesley, and Roy A. Adkins. *Handbook to Life in Ancient Rome*. Oxford: Oxford University Press, 1998.

Alston, Richard. *Aspects of Roman History: A. D. 14–117*. New York: Routledge, 1998.

Badolato, Francesco, and Pierre Coustillas. 1997. "Gissing and the Paparazzi." *The Gissing Journal*, Vol. XXXIII, No. 4 (October 1997).

Badolato, Francesco, and Pierre Coustillas. 1998. "More About Gissing and the Paparazzi." *The Gissing Journal*, Vol. XXXIV, No. 1 (January 1998).

Barzini, Luigi. *The Italians*. New York: Atheneum, 1964.

Blanchard, Paul. Blue Guide. *Southern Italy: South of Rome to Calabria*. London: A. & C. Black (Publishers) Ltd., 1996.

Boardman, John. *The Greeks Overseas*. Baltimore: Penguin Books, 1964.

Brook, Clifford. Introduction by Pierre Coustillas. *George Gissing and Wakefield*. Wakefield: Wakefield Historical Publications and The Gissing Trust, 1992.

Bullitt, Orville H. *Search for Sybaris*. Philadelphia: J. B. Lippincott Co., 1969.

Bury, J. B. *History of the Later Roman Empire*. 2 vols. New York: Dover Publications Inc., 1958.

Select Bibliography

Clark, Martin. *The Italian Risorgimento.* New York: Addison-Wesley Longman Inc., 1998.

Clifton, Harry. *On the Spine of Italy: A Year in the Abruzzi.* London: Macmillan Publishers, Ltd., 1999.

Coustillas, Pierre, ed. *London and the Life of Literature in Late Victorian England: The Diary of George Gissing, Novelist.* Hassocks, Sussex, England: Harrester Press, Ltd., 1978.

Curtis, Anthony. "A Visit to Bee Bee." *The Gissing Journal,* Vol. XXXV, No. 2 (April 1999).

Dimitriadou, Maria. "Greek Culture and Gissing's Journey to Greece." *The Gissing Journal,* Vol. XXXIV, No. 4 (October 1998).

Douglas, Norman. *Old Calabria.* Marlboro, Vt.: The Marlboro Press, 1993.

Dragone, Sergio. *Catanzaro: I luoghi, le persone, la storia.* Catanzaro: Cinesud Due Editore, 1994.

Dunne, Brian Ború. Paul F. Mattheisen, Arthur C. Young, and Pierre Coustillas, eds. *With Gissing in Italy: The Memoirs of Brian Ború Dunne.* Athens, Ohio: Ohio University Press, 1999.

Finely, M. I. *Atlas of Classical Archaeology.* New York: McGraw-Hill Book Co., 1977.

Gibbon, Edward. *The Decline and Fall of the Roman Empire.* New York. Penguin Books USA, 1985.

Gissing, George. *By the Ionian Sea: Notes of a Ramble in Southern Italy.* London: Chapman and Hall Ltd., 1901.

———. *By the Ionian Sea.* London: Century Hutchinson Ltd., Brookmount House, 1986.

———. *The Private Papers of Henry Ryecroft.* New York: Signet, 1961.

———. *Veranilda: An Unfinished Romance.* Oxford: Oxford University Press, 1929.

Grant, Michael. *The Collapse and Recovery of the Roman Empire.* New York: Routledge, 1999.

Guido, Margaret. *Southern Italy: An Archaeological Guide to the Main Prehistoric, Greek and Roman Sites.* Park Ridge, N.J.: Noyes Press, 1973.

Haydock, James. *Portraits in Charcoal: George Gissing's Image of Women.* Gissing Resources on the Internet, 1998.

Herodotus. *The Histories.* Translated by Robin Waterfield. Oxford: Oxford University Press, 1998.

Holmes, George, ed. *The Oxford History of Italy.* Oxford: Oxford University Press, 1997.

Horace. *Odes & Epodes.* Translated by Joseph P. Clancy. Chicago: The University of Chicago Press, 1971.

Hornblower, Simon, and Anthony Spawforth. *The Oxford Classical Dictionary.* Oxford: Oxford University Press, 1996.

Hornblower, Simon, and Anthony Spawforth. *The Oxford Companion to Classical Civilization.* Oxford: Oxford University Press, 1998.

Korg, Jacob. *George Gissing: A Critical Biography.* London: Methuen & Co. Ltd., 1965.

Levi, Carlo. *Christ Stopped at Eboli.* New York: Farrar, Straus and Giroux, 1987.

Livy. *The War with Hannibal: Books XXI–XXX of The History of Rome from Its Foundation.* Translated by Aubrey de Sélincourt. Edited with an introduction by Betty Radice. London: Penguin Books Ltd., 1972.

Marrone, Romualdo. *Le Strade di Napoli (The Roads of Naples).* Rome: Newton Compton, 1996.

Máté, Ferenc. *The Hills of Tuscany: A New Life in an Old Land.* New York: W. W. Norton, 1998.

Mattheisen, Paul F., Arthur C. Young, and Pierre Coustillas, eds. *The Collected Letters of George Gissing.* 9 vols. Athens, Ohio: Ohio University Press, 1990–1997.

Mayes, Frances. *Bella Tuscany.* New York: Broadway Books, 1999.

Mayes, Frances. *Under the Tuscan Sun: At Home in Italy.* New York: Broadway Books, 1997.

Morkot, Robert. *The Penguin Historical Atlas of Ancient Greece.* London: Penguin Books Ltd., 1996.

Morton, H. V. *A Traveller in Southern Italy.* New York: Dodd, Mead & Company, 1969.

Select Bibliography

Morton, Peter. The George Gissing Web Site. Flinders University of South Australia. 1998.

Newby, Eric. *A Small Place in Italy*. Hawthorn, Australia: Lonely Planet Publications, 1998.

Newby, Eric. *Love and War in the Apennines*. Hawthorn, Australia: Lonely Planet Publications, 1999.

Paolicelli, Paul. *Dances with Luigi*. New York: Thomas Dunne Books, St. Martin's Press, 2000.

Peddie, John. *Hannibal's War*. Phoenix Mill: Sutton Publishing Ltd., 1997.

Robb, Peter. *Midnight in Sicily: On Art, Food, History, Travel & La Cosa Nostra*. Winchester, Mass.: Faber and Faber Inc., 1998.

Romm, James. *Herodotus*. New Haven: Yale University Press, 1998.

Stille, Alexander. *Excellent Cadavers: The Mafia and the Death of the First Italian Republic*. New York: Vintage, 1996.

Touring Club Italiano. *Atlante Stradale Touring—Italy*. Milan: Rotolito Lombarda S.p.A., 1995.

Troiano, Giovanni. Illus. *Sybaris: History and Myth: Guide to the Archaeological Excavation of Sybaris and the National Archaeological Sibaritide Museum*. Galasso Editore, 1997.

Tullio, Paolo. *North of Naples, South of Rome*. New York: Thomas Dunne Books, St. Martin's Press, 1998.